The First

American Frontier

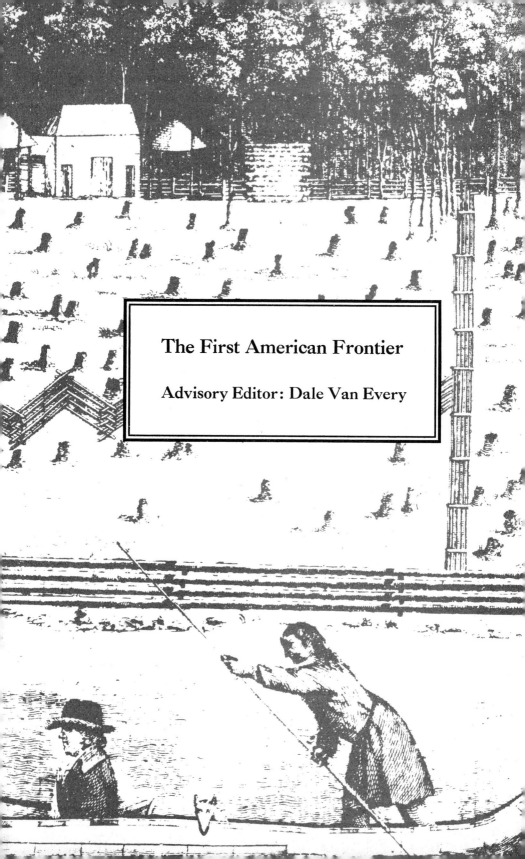

The First American Frontier

Advisory Editor: Dale Van Every

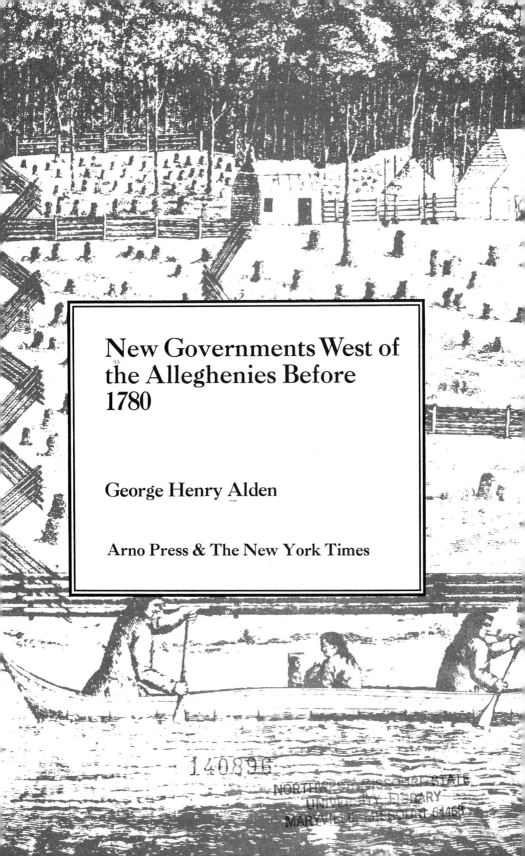

New Governments West of the Alleghenies Before 1780

George Henry Alden

Arno Press & The New York Times

Reprint Edition 1971 by Arno Press Inc.

Reprinted from a copy in
The State Historical Society of Wisconsin Library

LC # 70-106117
ISBN 0-405-02822-9

The First American Frontier
ISBN for complete set: 0-405-02820-2

See last pages of this volume for titles.

Manufactured in the United States of America

BULLETIN OF THE UNIVERSITY OF WISCONSIN

HISTORICAL SERIES, VOL. 2, NO. 1, PP. 1-74.

NEW GOVERNMENTS WEST OF THE ALLEGHANIES
BEFORE 1780.

(INTRODUCTORY TO A STUDY OF THE ORGANIZATION AND
ADMISSION OF NEW STATES.)

BY

GEORGE HENRY ALDEN.

Acting Assistant Professor of History, University of Illinois.

*A Thesis submitted for the degree of Doctor of Philosophy in the
Department of History.*

PUBLISHED BY AUTHORITY OF LAW AND WITH THE APPROVAL OF
THE REGENTS OF THE UNIVERSITY

MADISON, WIS.
PUBLISHED BY THE UNIVERSITY
APRIL, 1897.

PREFACE.

When this study was begun in the Seminary of American History and Institutions at Harvard University it was my intention to cover the ground occupied by this monograph in a very few pages, but as the work advanced it became apparent that so short a treatment of the early period would be quite inadequate. Gradually my introduction to the larger study on the establishment and admission of new states assumed this present form.

In the following pages I have aimed to give a fair account of the early attempts to make new governmental establishments in the West, and to show the attitude of the British government toward such establishments. The available data in regard to British policy are not as full as could be desired, but I have tried to judge them fairly and they seem to me sufficient to warrant the conclusions drawn. That there were movements which led the way to the subsequent cutting up of the West into new states, has I think, been made clear.

The materials upon which this paper is based were collected in the Harvard University library and in the library of the Wisconsin State Historical Society. In the latter I found especially valuable the Draper Collection of MSS., to which, by the courtesy of Secretary Reuben G. Thwaites, I had free access.

I desire to express obligations to Professor Albert Bushnell Hart, of Harvard University, by whose sugges-

tion and inspiration I began this study. Professor Victor
Coffin, of the University of Wisconsin, and Professor
Evarts B. Greene, of the University of Illinois, have given
me helpful suggestions. But more than to all others
are my thanks due to Professor Frederick J. Turner, the
editor of this series, who, by his kindly criticism, helped
me to bring this paper to its present form.

GEORGE H. ALDEN.

TABLE OF CONTENTS.

PAGE.

CHAPTER I.—SCHEMES FOR NEW COLONIES PRIOR TO 1766 1

1. Land Companies (Introductory) 2
2. The Albany Plan 3
3. Franklin's Proposition 3
4. Pownall's Proposition 5
5. Hazard's Scheme 7
6. Pittsylvania 12
7. Charlotiana 12
8. Charles Lee's Proposition 14

CHAPTER II.—THE ILLINOIS AND VANDALIA PROJECTS.

1. Scheme for colonies at Detroit and on the Illinois and Ohio 16
2. Vandalia 19
   a. Petition for Land Grant 20
   b. A Government Suggested 21
   c. Correspondence with Virginian Authorities 22
   d. Hillsborough's Report and Franklin's Reply 23
   e. Report of Council Committee, July 1, 1772. 26
   f. The King's Approval and Orders to Board of Trade, Aug. 14, 1772 27
   g. Lord Dartmouth's Report, May 6, 1773.. 28
      (a.) Form of Government 29
      (b.) Boundaries 31
   h. The Papers Prepared 34
   i. The Final Failure 35

PAGE.

CHAPTER III.— CONCLUSIONS FROM THE FOREGOING CHAPTERS.

1.	Most Schemes to Locate on the Ohio.........	36
2.	People Interested are Mostly from Pennsylvania and New Jersey	36
3.	King's Right to cut off Old Colonies Conceded.	37
4.	Attitude of the British Government	38
	a. Administration of Colonial Affairs.......	38
	b. Personal Influence of Hillsborough......	39
	c. Settlement Encouraged in 1748..........	41
	d. Proclamation of 1763...................	42
	e. Illinois Scheme in Favor till 1768........	45
	f. Defeat of Illinois Scheme................	45
	g. Purchase from the Six Nations..........	45
	h. Vandalia..............................	46
	i. Policy not to be Expected Consistent....	46
	j. But on the Whole not Unfavorable to Western Colonies.....................	47
	k. The West in a Fair Way to Being Cut into New Colonies...................	48

CHAPTER IV.— TRANSYLVANIA.

1.	Probable Intention to get a Crown Grant......	49
2.	Membership of the Company.................	50
3.	Boundaries	51
4.	Dunmore's Opposition	54
5.	The "Plan" of Government.................	55
6.	Session of the "Convention"..................	56
7.	Delegate and Memorial to Congress...........	57
8.	Attitude of Members of Congress.............	57
9.	Settlers' Petition to Virginia..................	58
10.	New "Convention" postponed...............	59
11.	Clark's Plan................................	60
12.	Delegates Elected to Virginia Assembly........	60
13.	Clark's Threat..............................	61
14.	Kentucky County Erected...................	61
15.	Probable Results had Kentucky Remained Independent............................	62

PAGE.

CHAPTER V.—NEW STATE SCHEMES PRIOR TO 1780.

      1. Westsylvania 64

           a. First movement, June, 1776 64

           b. Petition to Congress 65

      2. Silas Deane's Suggestion 68

      3. General Conclusion 69

BIBLIOGRAPHY.

LIST OF MAPS.

Hazard's Scheme 9

Charlotiana 13

Vandalia 33

Transylvania 53

Westsylvania 67

NEW GOVERNMENTS WEST OF THE ALLEGHANIES BEFORE 1780.

CHAPTER I.

SCHEMES FOR NEW COLONIES PRIOR TO 1766.

The English colonies in America remained for a century after their establishment in practical ignorance of the land beyond the Alleghany mountains. There was land enough nearer the coast and why should the settler advance be yond that forbidding line which separated civilization from the unknown and desolate wilderness? In 1716, how-ever, Governor Spotswood made his famous ride over the Blue Ridge and made known to Virginians the beauty and fertility of the valley of Virginia. Twenty-two years later Augusta county was created by the Virginia assembly, bounded on the east by the Blue Ridge, and west and northwest by "the utmost limits of Virginia."[1] This marks the first step towards establishing English colonial government west of the mountains.[2] With the increase of population on the seaboard came an increase in the num-ber of settlers' cabins beyond the mountains; and the in-creasing interest in western settlement was accompanied

---

[1] Hening, V., 79.

[2] In 1718, Sir William Keith, in a report to the Commissioners of Trade (Collection of Papers and other Tracts, p. 196), recommended the establishment of four small inland forts to protect the Indian trade. There was, however, no suggestion of a civil govern-ment in connection with them. About the same time Governor Spotswood of Virginia "laid an excellent scheme for extending that trade, and raising fortifications even on the banks of the Lake Erie." It is possible that this plan contemplated the planting of a civil government in the West, but there is no evidence of it. See State of the British and French Cols. in N. Am., p. 109. Cf. Spotswood Letters.

by the formation of great land companies, the Ohio Company leading the way in 1747, and obtaining, two years later, a grant of 500,000 acres. In the official instructions to the governor of Virginia in regard to this company, sent doubtless by Lord Halifax, then president of the board of trade, it is set forth that " such settlements will be for our interest, . . . inasmuch as our loving subjects will be thereby enabled to cultivate a friendship, and carry on a more extensive commerce with the nations of Indians inhabiting those parts: and such examples may likewise induce the neighboring colonies to turn their thoughts towards designs of the same nature."[1] The grant was located between the Monongahela and Kanawha rivers on both sides of the Ohio.[2]

In the same year was organized the Loyal Company, which obtained a grant of 800,000 acres.

Encouraged, doubtless, by the apparent ease with which these two, and other companies secured their extensive grants from the crown,[3] and by the expressed attitude of the British government towards western settlement, many schemes were brought forward during the next quarter century for securing similar grants. There seemed to be almost an epidemic of interest aroused in western lands, and new colonial governments, which it was proposed, in many instances to establish.

Probably the earliest public proposition for new colonial governments beyond the mountains of which record remains, was that set forth by the Albany congress of 1754.[4] The

[1] Franklin's Works, V., 33.

[2] Dinwiddie papers, I., 17, note. Holmes says the Ohio Company's grant comprised 600,000 acres. Am. Annals, II., 39.

[3] That the grants were given by direct order from His Majesty, is shown by letter of Gov. Dinwiddie to Gov. Glenn,—Dinwiddie Papers I., 272; also by S. Sato, Land Question in the U. S., p. 25. Sato gives a good account of the various land companies, pp. 24-25, for which see also Perkins, Annals of the West, pp. 50, 52, 106, 108, 109, 135, 177.

[4] In 1730 Joshua Gee (The Trade and Navigation of Great Britain Considered, p. 61) wrote concerning the land " back of all our settlements " as follows: " If we have any Sense of the Value of that commodious Tract of Land, it ought to put us upon securing to ourselves such excellent Colonies, which may, if properly improved, bring this

Plan of Union proposed by that Congress, provided that the President General and Grand Council should make all purchases of Indian lands and establish settlements upon them; and also "That they make laws for regulating and governing such new settlements till the crown shall think fit to form them into particular governments."[1] Dr. Franklin, in his notes on the Plan says: "A particular colony has scarce strength enough to extend itself by new settlements at so great a distance from the old; but the joint force of the Union might suddenly establish a new colony or two in those parts . . greatly to the security of our present frontiers, increase of trade and people. . . . The power of settling new colonies is, therefore, thought a valuable part of the plan."[2]

Soon after the Albany Congress, Franklin proposes a somewhat definite scheme for two new colonies to be located between the Ohio and Lake Erie. Some of the details are interesting, as showing Franklin's general idea of establishing new colonies. He begins by reciting the advantages to be expected from the establishment of the proposed colonies by way of protection to the frontiers, vantage ground from which to attack the French, and secure friendship and trade with the Indians, besides facilitating English settlement to the Mississippi and Great Lakes. If the old colonies were united "agreeably to the Albany plan they might easily, by their joint force, establish one or more new colonies.   . . But if such union should not

---

Nation a very great Treasure, and at least build some Forts upon the Apulachean Mountains, to secure us the Right of the Mines contained in them, to protect the Indian and skin Trade." It is just possible to take the expression "such excellent colonies," etc., to refer to new colonies; but from the context it seems more probable that the old colonies are referred to, they being already somewhat menaced by the advance of the French in the west.

[1] Franklin's Works, II., 368. (Unless otherwise stated all references to Franklin's Works are to the Bigelow edition.)

[2] Franklin's Works, II., 368. Franklin, in the same connection, also advocated the establishment of forts on the great lakes and the Ohio, as they would not only secure the frontiers but "serve to defend new colonies settled under their protection; and such colonies would also mutually defend and support such forts, and better secure the friendship of the far Indians."

take place it is proposed that two charters be granted, each for some considerable part of the lands west of Pennsylvania and the Virginia mountains, to a number of the nobility and gentry of Britain with such Americans as shall join them in contributing to the settlement of those lands." In regard to the government of his proposed colonies, Franklin suggests "that as many and as great privileges and powers of government be granted to the contributors and settlers as his Majesty in his wisdom shall think most fit for their benefit and encouragement, consistent with the general good of the British empire; for extraordinary privileges and liberties, with lands on easy terms, are strong inducements to people to hazard their persons and fortunes in settling new countries. And such powers of government as (though suitable to their circumstances and fit to be trusted with an infant colony) might be judged unfit when it becomes populous and powerful, these might be granted for a term only, as the choice of their own governor for 99 years; the support of government in the colonies of Connecticut and Rhode Island (which now enjoy that and other like privileges) being much less expensive than in colonies under the immediate government of the crown, and the constitution more inviting."[1] Franklin recurs again to his idea of establishing forts to protect the new colonies. A fort at Buffalo Creek on the Ohio, "and another at the mouth of the Tioga, on the south side of Lake Erie," would protect one colony. This is all the clue he gives us as to its location. He is a little more definite in regard to the other. He says, "The river Scioto . . . is supposed the fittest seat for the other colony, there being for forty miles on each side of it, and quite up to its head, a body of all rich land."[2] We may infer then that Franklin would locate one of his colonies in what is now northwestern Pennsylvania, and northeastern Ohio, and the

---

[1] For the scheme in full see Franklin's Works, II., 474.

[2] Franklin adds that this is "the finest spot of its bigness in all North America, and has the particular advantage of sea-coal in plenty."

other on the Ohio river, extending it northwards on both
sides of the Scioto. Evidently the exact location of new
colonies is a minor question with him at this time. But
now, as afterwards, he is quite desirous to have western
colonies established and wants to have a part in their
establishment himself. In 1756 he wrote to Rev. George
Whitfield: "I sometimes wish that you and I were jointly
employed by the crown to settle a colony on the Ohio. I
imagine that we could do it effectually, and without putting the nation to much expense; but I fear we shall never
be called upon for such a service. What a glorious thing
it would be to settle in that fine country a large, strong
body of religious and industrious people! What a security
to the other colonies and advantage to Britain, by increasing her people, territory, strength, and commerce. Might
it not greatly facilitate the introduction of pure religion
among the heathen, if we could, by such a colony, show
them a better sample of Christians than they commonly
see in our Indian traders? — the most vicious and abandoned wretches of our nation!" [1]

But Franklin was not the only prominent man to advocate new colonies at that time. Thomas Pownall had been
a member of the Albany Congress, and Lieutenant Governor of New Jersey. By order of the Duke of Cumberland
he drew up in 1756, " A Memorial: Stating the nature
of the service in North America, and proposing a General
plan of operations, as founded thereon." [2] He inserts
Franklin's scheme as well as one of his own.

Barrier colonies are advocated by Thomas Pownall. In
his memorial he says: . . . "wherever our settlements
have been wisely and completely made, the French, neither
by themselves, nor their dogs of war, the Indians, have been
able to remove us. It is upon this fact that I found the
propriety of the measure of settling a barrier colony in

---

[1] Franklin's Works, II., 467.

[2] Pownall, Administration of the Colonies, Appendix, p. 47.

those parts of our frontiers which are not the immediate residence or hunting grounds of our Indians. This is a measure that will be effectual, and will not only in time pay its expence, but make as great returns as any of our present colonies do; will give a strength and unity to our dominions in North America, and give us possession of the country as well as settlements in it. But above all this the state and circumstances of our settlements render such a measure not only proper and eligible, but absolutely necessary. The English settlements, as they are at present circumstanced, are absolutely at a stand; they are settled up to the mountains, and in the mountains there is nowhere together land sufficient for a settlement large enough to subsist by itself and to defend itself, and preserve a communication with the present settlements. If the English would advance one step further, or cover themselves where they are, it must be at once, by one large step over the mountains with a numerous and military colony. Where such should be settled, I do not now take upon me to say; at present I shall only point out the measure and the nature of it, by inserting two schemes, one of Mr. Franklin's; the other of your memorialist; and if I might indulge myself with scheming, I should imagine that two such were sufficient, and only requisite and proper; one at the back of Virginia, filling up the vacant space between the Five Nations and southern confederacy, and connecting into a one system, our barrier. The other somewhere in the Cohass on Connecticut river; or wherever best adapted to cover the four New England Colonies. " Further details of Pownall's scheme do not appear. It is noticeable that the location back of Virginia which he advises for one colony was afterwards taken by the Walpole company, of which he was a member. It is noticeable, too, that Pownall's scheme, as well as Franklin's, provides for more than one colony, each to cover apparently no very large extent of territory. If one or two small colonies had been established west of the mountains, the establishment of others would easily follow until the whole western country was cut up into colonies. In prominent circles, therefore, back colonies were being considered.

The Albany congress had discussed a plan of union which contemplated the establishment of back colonies; Franklin was exhibiting a great interest in the subject, and was bringing forward more or less definite plans; Thomas Pownall, ready himself with certain propositions for new colonies, was bringing the matter to the attention of the King's brother, the Duke of Cumberland, in a memorial upon colonial administration prepared by order of his royal highness himself. Nor was there a lack of interest on the part of less prominent people. Samuel Hazard, a merchant of Philadelphia, had projected a scheme for a new colony beyond the mountains, and by the spring of 1755, had engaged over 3,500 persons "able to bear arms, to remove to the said new Colony, on the footing of said scheme, and does not in the least doubt of being able to procure 10,000 if it takes effect."[1] He declared then that "among those already engaged are nine Reverend Ministers of the Gospel, a considerable number of persons who are in public offices under the governments of Pennsylvania and New Jersey, as well as great numbers of persons of good estates, of the best characters for sobriety and religion in said provinces, but more especially in the Province of Pennsylvania." Hazard proposed to get "a Grant of so much Land as shall be necessary for the Settlement of an ample colony, to begin at the distance of one hundred miles westward of the Western Boundaries of Pennsylvania, and thence to extend one Hundred Miles to the westward of the River Mississippi, and to be divided from Virginia and Carolina by the Great Chain of Mountains that runs along the Continent from the North Eastern to the South Western Parts of America."[2]

[1] Hazard's petition to the General Assembly of Connecticut, 4 Amer. Archives, I., 863.
[2] Hazard's whole "Scheme" may be found in 4 Amer. Archives, I., 861, and in Christopher Gist's Journal, 261. In the latter, however, no hundred mile interval is proposed west of the limits of Pennsylvania.

This does not indicate the proposed extent from north to south, unless, indeed, we consider that extent to be indicated by the length of the designated boundary on the east, i. e., from Pennsylvania to Carolina inclusive.[1] That would certainly be "an ample colony" which embraced all the Ohio, and a large part of the Mississippi valleys. Whether it was expected that this colony would be divided and subdivided as it increased in population and diversity of interests we do not know. It is not impossible that the petitioners had little idea of the extent of the territory indicated, as little was commonly known about it at that time.

It was proposed "That humble Application be made to His Majesty for a Charter to erect said Territory into a separate Government, with the same Privileges which the Colony of Connecticut enjoys," and "That application be made to the Assemblies of the several British Colonies in North America to grant such Supplies of Money and Provisions as may enable the Settlers to secure the Friendship of the Indian Natives, and support themselves and Families till they are established."

There is evidence that the design was to establish a Presbyterian colony.[2] Certainly the religious element was to be very prominent. Only Protestants believing in the divine authority of the Old and New Testaments and the trinity of the Godhead, and with lives and conversations free from immorality and profaneness, could hold office. Roman Catholics were debarred from holding land or having arms or ammunition in their possession, "nor shall any Mass Houses or Popish Chappels be allowed in the Province."

[1] This view is supported by the fact that in the fall of 1755 he made a journey, probably of investigation, "chiefly on the frontiers of Pennsylvania, Maryland, Virginia and North Carolina." Hazard to Pownall, Almon's Remembrancer, III., 133.

[2] The petition to Connecticut recites that New England, having lands of her own to settle, a new colony would be able to obtain recruits that could be depended upon for fidelity to the king only among members of the Church of England, the Presbyterians, Quakers, and Baptists. The Church of England had shown no disposition to settle colonies in the wilderness. Quakers would not go because "principled against war to remove and defend the country." Baptists were too few. So Presbyterians only remained by whom a new colony could be settled. 4 Amer. Archives, I., 863.

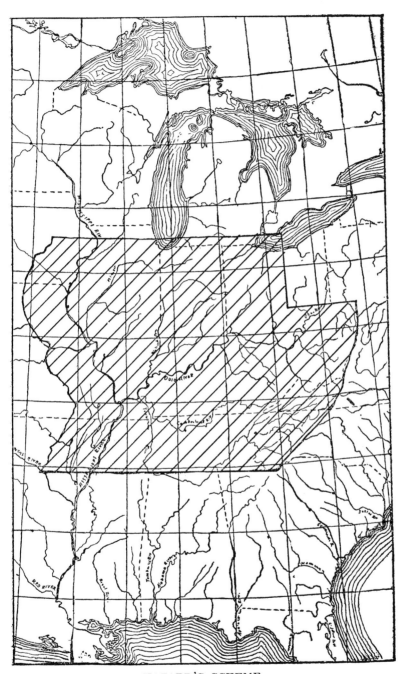

HAZARD'S SCHEME.

The above will sufficiently show what Hazard's plan was. Having drawn up his "Scheme" and being assured of colonists to undertake the settlement, of course his next step was to endeavor to secure the grant. The design seems to have been at one time to petition the General Assembly of Connecticut "to make Application to His Majesty for a Charter" in behalf of the would-be colonists,[1] but it was finally decided to ask Connecticut for nothing more than a relinquishment of her claims upon the desired lands. In May, 1755, a petition to that effect was presented to the General Assembly, and was granted on condition that "the Petitioner obtain his Majesty's Royal Grant and order for settling the said Colony."[2] Hazard's son relates that his father, after getting this relinquishment from Connecticut, "procured the subscription of between four and five thousand persons, able to bear arms, some of whom were worth thousands,— that he personally explored that part of the country proposed for the situation of the new colony; that he had corresponded with some of the nobility, and with other persons of note and influence in England, who appear to have favoured and encouraged the design; and that having, as he apprehended, brought the scheme to a proper degree of maturity, he proposed embarking for England in the fall of the year, 1758, in order to procure its final accomplishment."[3] A petition to the king said there was no doubt that the "Royal wisdom and penetration has discovered the necessity and importance of settling strong and numerous

---

[1] See the petition in Christopher Gist's Journal, p. 266, "To the Honourable the Governor, Council and Representatives of the Colony of Connecticut," to which " were affixed more than two thousand names."

[2] Colonial Records of Conn., X., 382, and 4 Am. Archives, I., 865.

[3] Memorial of Ebenezer Hazard of New York, 1774, in 4 Am. Archives, I., 865. The son goes on to say that his father's death left the associates " without a guide sufficient to conduct so important an enterprise," but that he himself proposes to take up the Scheme and make "a settlement under the claim and jurisdiction of the colony of Connecticut," so as " not to be obliged to carry the matter to England." He offers to Connecticut £10,000 for the land which he proposes to bound on the west by the Mississippi, and on the east by the western boundary of Pennsylvania. The Connecticut General Assembly, however, rejected his offer, and we hear nothing more of the Hazard Scheme.

Colonies in the neighborhood of the Ohio and Mississippi,"
and prayed for "such countenance and assistance . . . as
will be necessary for the encouragement of a people on
whose fidelity your Majesty may with the utmost confidence
rely, and who, at the same time, esteem themselves bound
by the most sacred and indissoluble ties, to hand down the
blessings of civil and religious liberty inviolate to their
posterity." [1] This was quite probably intended as a plea
for a charter granting a liberal government. Such was what
he desired, for we find him writing to Thomas Pownall as
follows: "Even the wildest anarchy could hardly be worse
than government managed as it frequently has been in the
colonies southward of New England. . . . If any schemes
be gone into for settling a new colony, I hope things will
be put on such a footing as will prevent those jars and con-
tentions between the different branches of the legislature
which have almost ruined some of the colonies." [2]

But enough has been said to show the main points of
Hazard's scheme.   Whether, if he had lived, he would
have succeeded in securing a grant of even a portion of
the territory asked for, we are of course unable to say.
He himself and his supporters doubtless had faith in the
success of the undertaking or they would not have proceeded so far in it as they did.   With his death in the summer of 1758 we hear nothing further of his attempt to
plant a new colonial government beyond the mountains.
In that same year, however, another proposition was made
for a new colony.

A few days after the capture of Fort Du Quesne a writer
from that place "suggested that the King should grant a
charter for a western colony 'with a full liberty of con-
science' and a separate governor; and another writer

---

[1] 4 Am. Archives, I., 863.

[2] Hazard to Pownall, Jan. 14, 1756, Almon's Remembrancer, III, 134. He tells Pownall
that "you will undoubtedly have an opportunity of communicating what has been done
to the Earl of Halifax, and such others at the head of affairs as you think proper."
This would indicate that Hazard expected assistance from Pownall.

shortly after proposed for it the name of Pittsylvania
. . . and that all Protestants who should come under the
denomination of King David's soldiers, mentioned by the
prophet Samuel, and that everyone that was in distress,
everyone that was in debt, and every one that was discon-
tented, should be invited to settle in that 'extraordinary
good land.' "[1] This seems to have indicated a movement to
establish a new colony from philanthropic motives. So far
as we know nothing ever came of the proposition.

With the close of the French and Indian war, projects
for new western colonies appeared faster, and now not only
in America but in Great Britain as well. A pamphlet was
published in London urging the "Advantages of a Settlement upon the Ohio in North America."[2] In the same
year there appeared in Edinburgh a pamphlet recommend-
ing "That Virginia, Maryland, and Pennsylvania be termin-
ated by a bound to be fixed thus: From Lake Erie, up the
river Miamis[3] to the Carrying-place, from thence down the
river Waback to where it runs into the Ohio, and from
thence down the Ohio to the Forks of the Mississippi."[4]
The author of the pamphlet further recommends "That the
country betwixt the Mississippi and the fresh-water Lakes,
extending northwest from this proposed bound, be formed
into a new Colony, which might be called Charlotiana, in
honour of Her Majesty, our present most excellent Queen."
It was urged that this location was the most fertile and
healthful in North America, and a town at or near the
"Forks of the Mississippi" would become "the common Em-
porium of the produce and riches of that vast continent."
A colony located there would give the British "the entire
command of that Continent", secure the Indian trade, and
defend the country and the old colonies from hostile French

---

[1] Draper Collection. Draper's MS. Life of Boone, III., 266, citing Maryland Gazette,
January 12, and March 22, 1759. For "King David's soldiers" see I Samuel, XXII, 2.

[2] Draper's MS. Life of Boone, III., 266.

[3] Now called the Maumee.

[4] Expediency of Securing our American Colonies, p. 13.

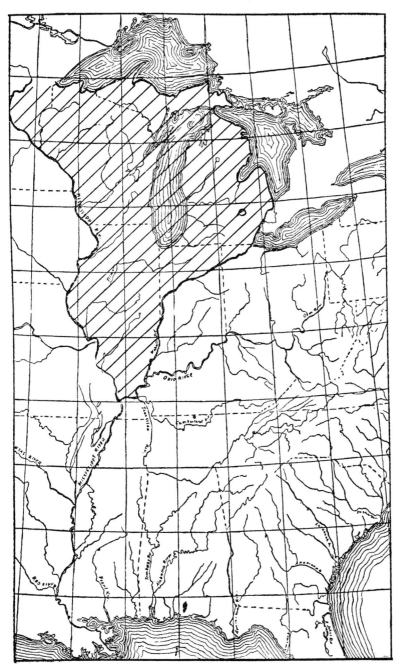

CHARLOTIANA.

or Indians.[1] It was advised that the new settlers be furnished "a stock of cattle, furniture, utensils" et cetera; that they be given lands on easy tenure; that they be given also "a set of well-contrived good rules with respect to their constitution, polity, œconomy and order, wise prudent Governors, and a sufficient number of able approven Clergymen and teachers."[2] It was thought that a new colony might easily be peopled with disbanded soldiers and sailors, poverty stricken farmers of England and Ireland, and unfortunate debtors then "pining in jails throughout Britain and Ireland" who could be liberated by the royal mercy on condition of removal to the Mississippi valley.[3] Masons, carpenters, joiners, and bricklayers would be necessary, and miners might be of good service also on account of the mines of silver, lead, and iron which were "said to be in great numbers and very rich" north of the Illinois.[4]

These are the main ideas of the scheme proposed in the Edinburgh pamphlet. It was urged that the new colony be erected at once so as to check Indian insurrections then in progress,[5] but the scheme seems never to have been considered by the British Government.[6]

About the same time Colonel Charles Lee proposed two new colonies. He suggested that one be located on the Illinois, and the other on the Ohio below the Wabash.[7]

The King's proclamation of 1763, declaring the western lands reserved "for the present" for the use of the Indians probably checked these and other movements toward western settlement. At all events we do not find a record of many attempts to found new colonies after that date. The

---

[1] Ibid, p. 16.

[2] Ibid, p. 43.

[3] Ibid, pp. 43–46.

[4] Ibid, p. 28.

[5] Ibid, p. 54.

[6] Lord Hillsborough, President of the Board of Trade, declared that the Illinois scheme of 1766–67 was the first one involving a new western colony that the government considered. See his report in Franklin's Works, V., 5 et seq.

[7] Draper, MS. Life of Boone, III., 266.

proclamation does not seem to be absolutely prohibitive however, as settlement is forbidden "without our special leave and license for that purpose first obtained."[1]

[1] For the Proclamation see Houston's Const. Docs. of Canada, p. 67, or Franklin's Works, V., 75.

CHAPTER II.

THE ILLINOIS AND VANDALIA PROJECTS.

Before three years had passed by, after the King's proclamation, another scheme for new colonies appeared and was presented for his Majesty's " special leave and license. "[1] The plan was drawn up by Governor William Franklin of New Jersey, with the approval of Sir William Johnson, British Superintendent of Indian Affairs.[2] If the scheme did not at first contemplate three new governments, it soon assumed that form. The seat of one was to be at Detroit, another in " the Illinois country " and a third " on the lower part of the River Ohio.[3] There were to have been 100 original or chief proprietors in each colony, and each of these proprietors was to have been allowed to take up 20,000 acres of land (without paying any fine or consideration to the King for them), and to sell to undertenants; and the proprietors were also to have possessed their lands fifteen years, without paying any quit-rent or taxes; . . .   at the expiration of the 15 years, they were to have paid a quit-rent to the King of two shillings per

---

[1] In May, 1755, General Lyman with 850 associates called the "Susquehannah Company" petitioned the General Assembly of Connecticut for western lands proposing to settle under Connecticut jurisdiction (Conn. Col. Rec. X. 378.) After the French and Indian War, General Lyman appears in London trying to get a crown grant (Franklin's Works, IV., 137 et seq.). It is quite possible that his scheme at that time involved a new colonial government, but I have no evidence to prove it. For an account of General Lyman and his schemes see Am. Hist. Assoc. Report, 1893, p. 333.

[2] Franklin to his son, Works IV., 141; and William Franklin to his father, Works (Sparks) VII., 355.

[3] Franklin's Works V., 45. In Considerations on the Agreement, with the Hon. Thos. Walpole (p. 21) notice the following: ". . . during the administration of the earl of Shelburne, several applications were made to his lordship, for grants of lands upon the River *Ohio, at the Illinois, and at Detroit;* and . . . his lordship, at that time proposed, the establishment of *three* new colonies at these places." The italics are not mine. The old pamphlet which is here and elsewhere quoted is an interesting and well written document that appeared in London in 1774. It is believed by Ford to have been written by Dr. Franklin. See his Bibliography of Franklin.

hundred acres;— and this quit-rent was to have been altogether applied to the payment of the contingencies of
the government."[1] These propositions were approved by
Lord Shelburne.[2] Further particulars in regard to details of these schemes do not appear.

The one to be erected in the Illinois country received
the most attention and seemed most likely of approval by
the government. The assistance of Dr. Franklin, then in
London, as agent for Pennsylvania, was enlisted. In letters to his son he reported progress with the ministry.
That progress cannot be better shown than by a few selec-
tions from those letters. The first one, referring to it was
written May 10, 1766. He said, "I like the project of a
colony in the Illinois country and will forward it to my
utmost here." September 27, 1766—"I have mentioned the
Illinois affair to Lord Shelburne.[3] His Lordship had read
your plan for establishing a colony there, recommended by
Sir William Johnson, and said it appeared to him a reasonable scheme." October 11, 1766 — "I was again with Lord
Shelburne a few days since, and said a good deal to him on
the affair of the Illinois settlement. He was pleased to say
he really approved of it; but intimated that every new proposed expense for America would meet with great difficulty,
the treasury being alarmed and astonished at the growing
charges there, and the heavy accounts and drafts continually brought in from thence." November 8, 1766 — "Mr.
Jackson[4] is now come to town. The ministry have asked
his opinion and advice on your plan of a colony in the Illinois, and he has just sent me to peruse his answer in writing, in which he warmly recommends it, and enforces it by
strong reasons; which gives me great pleasure, as it cor-
roborates what I have been saying on the same topic, and

---

[1] Considerations on the Agreement . . with the Hon. Thos. Walpole, p. 22.

[2] Ibid.

[3] Lord Shelburne was at this time, and until 1768, Secretary of State for the southern
department.

[4] Richard Jackson was regularly appointed counsel to the Board of Trade in April,
1770. Chalmers, Opinions of Eminent Lawyers, p. 37.

from him appears less to be suspected of some American bias." June 13, 1767 — "The Illinois affair goes forward but slowly. Lord Shelburne told me again last week that he highly approved of it, but others were not of his sentiments, particularly the Board of Trade." August 28, 1767—"*The secretaries appeared finally to be fully convinced*, and there remained no obstacle but the Board of Trade, which was to be brought over privately before the matter should be referred to them officially. In case of laying aside the superintendents, a provision was thought of for Sir William Johnson. He will be made governor of the new colony."[1]   October 9, 1767—"I returned last night from Paris and just now hear that the Ilinois settlement is approved of in the Cabinet Council, so far as to be referred to the Board of Trade for their opinion."

November 13, 1767—"Since my return the affair of the Illinois settlement has been renewed. The King in Council referred the proposal to the Board of Trade, who called for the opinion of the merchants on two points, namely, whether the settlement of colonies in the Illinois country and at Detroit might not contribute to promote and extend the commerce of Great Britain; and whether the regulation of Indian trade might not best be left to the several colonies that carry on such trade; both which questions they considered at a meeting where Mr. Jackson and I were present, and *answered in the affirmative unanimously*, delivering their report accordingly to the Board."

November 25, 1767, at dinner with Lord Shelburne. "Among other things. . . . . we talked of the new settlements. *His Lordship told me he had himself drawn up a paper of reasons for those settlements* which he had laid be-

---

[1] In this same letter Franklin reports having a long conversation with Lord Shelburne and Mr. Conway, and urging the advantages of a settlement in the Illinois country in "securing the country, retaining the trade, raising a strength there which, on occasions of a future war, might easily be poured down the Mississippi upon the lower country, and into the Bay of Mexico, to be used against Cuba, the French Islands, or Mexico tself."

fore the King in Council. . . . . I think he added
that the Council seemed to approve of the design; I know
it was referred to the Board of Trade, who, I believe, have
not yet reported on it, and *I doubt will report against it.* . .
I waited next morning on Lord Clare. . . . We then
talked of the new colonies. I found he was inclined to
think one near the mouth of the Ohio might be of use in
securing the country, but did not much approve that at
Detroit. And, as to the trade, he imagined it would be of
little consequence, if we had it all, but supposed our traders would sell the peltry chiefly to the French and Spaniards at new Orleans, as he heard they had hitherto done."
March 13, 1768 — "The purpose of settling the new colonies
seems at present to be dropt, the change of American administration not appearing favorable to it. There seems
rather to be an inclination to abandon the posts in the back
country, as more expensive than useful. But counsels
are so continually fluctuating here that nothing can be depended on."[1]

Being Franklin's private messages to his son, these letters
doubtless show, as little else can, the true condition of
affairs in British governmental circles of the time, so
far as the question of new colonies is concerned. As for
new colonies in the Illinois country "the purpose of settling" them seems never to have been revived.[2] The new
Walpole or Vandalia company,[3] as it eventually came to be
called,[4] enlisted Franklin's energies instead, and as a member
of this company he made his most successful efforts to establish a British colonial government west of the Alleghany
mountains. This company's attempt is much more impor-

---

[1] These letters may be found in Franklin's Works, IV., 136-145. The italics are mine.

[2] See report of Board of Trade against the scheme, made in March, 1768, in Franklin's Works, V., 5 et seq.

[3] Some writers who speak of this company fail to distinguish it from the Illinois company. That they were two distinct companies may be seen by Franklin's letter to his
son (Works, IV., 138), Thos. Pownall to Sir Wm. Johnson, (Washington's Writings, II.,
328), and Plain Facts, p. 149.

[4] It was also named the "Grand Ohio Company." Christopher Gist's Journal, p. 243.

tant than any scheme thus far presented, not only because
of the attention which it attracted at the time,[1] but for the
fact, as it will be attempted to show, that in this case the
scheme finally met the approval of the British government
and, in obedience to that government's order, the papers
were actually drawn up for the establishment of a new
colony.

After the Six Nations had ceded to the crown in 1768 a
vast tract of land south of the Ohio,[2] a company was formed
in London for the purpose of endeavoring to buy a part of
it from the king.[3] It was composed of gentlemen residing
both in England and America. Thomas Walpole, Dr.
Franklin, John Sargent, and Samuel Wharton[4] were appointed a committee to manage the application for a land
grant. In June, 1769, these gentleman presented a petition
to his Majesty for the purchase of 2,400,000 acres. The
petition was referred to the Board of Trade, at the head of
which, was the Earl of Hillsborough. Mr Walpole and his
associates waited upon the Board of Trade in December,
1769, "when the Earl of Hillsborough recommended to
them to contract if possible with the lords of the Treasury
for such part of the purchase from the Six Nations, lying

---

[1] See the newspapers of 1772 and 1773.

[2] The treaty of Fort Stanwix, Nov. 5, 1768. The Indians ceded everything south of a
line "beginning at the Mouth of the Cherokee or Hogohege [Tennessee] river, where it
emptys into the River Ohio, and running from thence upwards along the South side of
said River to Kittaning, which is above Fort Pitt; from thence by a direct Line to the
nearest Fork of the west branch of Susquehanna, thence through the Alleghany Mountains . . ." Deed of cession, Docs. Rel. to Col. Hist. of the State of N. Y., VIII., 136.

[3] Plain Facts, p. 149. The pamphlet here cited appeared anonymously in Philadelphia in 1781. Its authorship is ascribed by Sabin (see his dictionary) to Dr.
Franklin or A. Benezêt. Much the same ground is covered without conflict in "Considerations upon the Agreement," and in Franklin's Reply to Hillsborough and
Memorial to Congress, from which we may judge the reliability as to facts of all of
them, even if Franklin were not the author of the anonymous pamphlets as is supposed.
Compare the proposals of Hoops and Buchanan, Feb. 22, 1769, in 4.Massachusetts Historical Collections, X., 608.

[4] Lord Camden, Thos. Pitt, Thos. Pownall, Sir William Johnson, and Colonel Croghan
were some of the other members of the Company. Plain Facts, p. 159; Considerations
on the Agreement, et cetera, p. 3, and letter of Thos. Pownall to Sir Wm. Johnson, April
1770, Washington's Writings, II., 328.

on the river Ohio, as would be sufficient in extent to form a separate government upon," [1] "promising them, in case of their agreement, *a good charter* for such government." [2]

"The Earl of Hillsborough offered to go immediately to the treasury and know their lordships opinion upon the subject, and the petitioners expressing their approbation, his lordship went, and reported that the lords of the treasury would be glad to receive the gentlemen's proposals." [3] This is the first definite suggestion of the idea of a new colonial government in connection with this scheme, and it i noticeable that the suggestion came in a very practical way, and from a man so prominent in the British government as the President of the Board of Trade. It is remarkable also in view of Lord Hillsborough's subsequent opposition to the new government which he himself suggested. [4] That Franklin, and perhaps his associates, had hoped to bring about in some way the establishment of a new government in connection with their scheme seems indeed very probable in the light of his previous interest in the question. However, the first petition of the Walpole company, as it was called, was for a comparatively small grant of land only, with apparently no thought of any new colonial government. [5] The larger tract of land suggested by Lord Hills-

[1] Plain Facts, p. 149.

[2] Considerations on the Agreement . . . with the Hon. Thomas Walpole, p. 2. The italics are not mine.

[3] Plain Facts, p. 149.

[4] Later Franklin wrote to his son concerning Lord Hillsborough as follows: "Witness, besides his various behaviour to me, his duplicity in encouraging us to ask for more land, *ask for enough to make a province* (when we at first asked only for 2,500,000 acres), were his words, pretending to befriend our application, then doing everything to defeat it; and reconciling the first to the last, by saying to a friend that he meant to defeat it from the beginning; and that his putting us upon asking so much was with that very view, supposing it too much to be granted." Franklin to his son, July 14, 1773 — Works, V., 196.

[5] Professor Hinsdale (Ohio Arch. and Hist. Quarterly, I., 218 and Old Northwest, p. 133) says that the proposition in 1769, was to establish a new colony and the petition was made for 2,400,000 acres "on which to found a new government." This is palpably an error. J. L. Peyton (Hist. of Augusta Co., Va., p. 144, et seq.) confuses the whole history of the Vandalia attempt with that of the Illinois scheme. Lord Fitzmaurice does the same, for he says that Shelburne " did his best to encourage the settlement on the Illinois known as Walpole's grant. "Life of Shelburne, II., 31.

borough was soon agreed upon with the lords of the Treasury, the price being £10,460: 7s: 3d., the amount paid the Six Nations for their cession.[1]

On the 8th of May, 1770, a petition for "a grant for the lands "[2] was presented to the King in council, by whom it was referred to the Board of Trade. July 15 following, Lord Hillsborough announced " that as there were, perhaps, some settlers from Virginia seated on part of the tract under consideration, he was of opinion that that colony should be acquainted with the contract made with the treasury; and therefore the report of the Lords of Trade would be delayed only until it was known whether Virginia had anything to say upon the subject."[3] The governor of Virginia, however, explained Lord Hillsborough, would be especially ordered to allow no surveys or settlements to be made " on any of the lands which the company had contracted for."

Governor Botetourt just having died,[5] Mr. Nelson, president of the Virginia council, replied officially October 18, 1770, to Lord Hillsborough's letter. He duly acknowledged the propriety and justice of "delaying to report in favour of Mr. Walpole and his associates for a grant of lands on the back of Virginia until the country should be made acquainted with it, and their reasons, if they had any, in objection should be heard."[5] Mr. Nelson hoped that the grants to the old Ohio company, to the officers of the late war, and to Colonel Croghan and the traders[6] would be re-

[1] Franklin's Works, V., 82.

[2] In April, 1770, Thomas Pownall wrote to Sir Wm. Johnson that a bargain with the treasury had been concluded for a large tract of land on the Ohio and that next an application would be made for a charter of government. Life and Writings of Washington (Sparks), II., 448. It would seem from this letter, as well as the subsequent history, that the petition was for a new government as well as for " a grant for the lands."

[3] Plain Facts, p. 150.

[4] Ibid., p. 159.

[5] Ibid., p. 152.

[6] Mr. Nelson estimated that these grants amounted altogether to about 1,700,000 acres. The author of Considerations on the Agreement estimated (p. 33) that with this deduction the Walpole company would have left "twelve millions of acres of cultivable lands." The traders' grant was provided for in the treaty of Fort Stanwix to compensate them for losses sustained in the French and Indian War. See Christopher Gist's Journal, p. 241; Plain Facts, p. 94.

spected, but he appears to have made no further objection. He said — " We do not presume to say to whom our gracious Sovereign shall grant his vacant lands; nor do I set myself up as an opponent to Mr. Walpole and his associates, . . . With respect to the establishment of a new colony on the back of Virginia, it is a subject of too great political importance for me to presume to give an opinion upon. However permit me, my Lord, to observe, that when that part of the country shall become sufficiently populated, it may be a wise and prudent measure." [1]

After nearly two years' delay the report of the Board of Trade appeared. It was a long argument against making the grant to Walpole and company, and called out a powerful and convincing reply from Dr. Franklin. [2] To the objection that the tract of land asked for " appears . . . to contain part of the dominion of Virginia . . . and to extend several degrees of longitude westward from the western ridge of the Appalachian Mountains," [3] he replied that " no part of the above tract is to the eastward of the Alleghany Mountains, and that those mountains must be considered the true western boundary of Virginia." [4]

Lord Hillsborough argued that part of the tract lay beyond the boundary line between his Majesty's territories and the Indian hunting grounds as established by treaties. [5] To this Franklin made a long argument to show that the treaty of Fort Stanwix vested in the crown the complete

---

[1] Plain Facts, p. 153, quoting Nelson's letter. Also Thos. Paine's Public Good, p. 24.

[2] Both documents may be found in Franklin's Works, V., 1-75. The President of the Board of Trade was Lord Hillsborough, who was also Secretary of State for the Colonies, an office created in 1768. The ministry rejecting his report, he " quit his American Seals, because he will not reconcile himself to a plan of settlement on the Ohio which all the world approves." Horace Walpole to Sir Horace Mann, July 23, 1772. Letters of Horace Walpole (Cunningham), V., 401. " Dr. Franklin's answer to the report of the Board of Trade was intended to have been published ; but, Lord Hillsborough resigning, Dr. Franklin stopped the sale on the morning of the publication when not above five copies had been disposed of ". Franklin's Works, X., 2.

[3] Franklin's Works, V., 3.

[4] Ibid., p. 20.

[5] Ibid., p. 3. Compare the treaty of Ft. Stanwix and the treaty of Lochaber, 1770. Cf. Massachusetts Historical Collections, X., 725.

title to all the lands asked for, and adds that if there has been
any agreement with the Indians not to allow settlement on
a part of them (which Franklin plainly doubts), that can
be easily arranged for " by a specific clause being inserted
into the King's grant to us, expressly prohibiting us from
settling any part of the same, until such time as we shall
have first obtained his Majesty's allowance and full consent of the Cherokees, and the Six Nations and their confederates for that purpose."[1]   In the third place it is urged
against the scheme that it is contrary to the principles
adopted by the Board "immediately after the treaty of
Paris, viz., the confining the western extent of settlements to
such a distance from the sea-coast as that those settlements
should lie within the reach of the trade and commerce of
this kingdom," not only for commercial purposes but also
to preserve " the colonies in due subordination to, and de-
pendence upon, the mother country."[2]   Against this, Franklin makes an argument to show that "the settlement of the
country over the Alleghany Mountains and on the Ohio was
not understood, either before the treaty of Paris, nor intended to be so considered by his Majesty's proclamation
of October, 1763, ' as without the reach of the trade and
commerce of this kingdom."[3]

To the argument that various propositions for erecting
colonies in the same part of the country have already been
rejected, and the same reasons for rejection exist in this
case, Franklin replies that, consistent with his knowledge,
"no more than one proposition for the settlement of any
of the land in question has been presented to government,
and that was from Dr. Lee " and thirty-four associates who
"did not propose, as we do, either to purchase the lands,
or pay the quit-rents to his Majesty, neat and clear of all

---

[1] Franklin's Works, V., 31.

[2] Lord Hillsborough adds here, "and these we apprehend to have been two capital
objects of his Majesty's proclamation of the 7th of October, 1763"—Ibid., p. 4.

[3] Ibid., p. 32.

deductions, or be at the whole expense of establishing and maintaining the civil government of the country."[1]

Hillsborough declared that "the great object of colonizing upon the continent of North America has been to improve and extend the commerce, navigation, and manufactures of this kingdom.

"(1) By promoting the advantageous fishery carried on upon the northern coast.

"(2) By encouraging the growth and culture of naval stores and of raw materials, to be transported hither in exchange for perfect manufactures and other merchandise.

"(3) By securing a supply of lumber, provisions, and other necessaries, for the support of our establishments in the American islands."[2]

Admitting this, Franklin asserts that the proposed "Ohio colony" will promote the fishery as much as any of the the colonies south of New York, and "on the second and third general reasons . . . no part of his Majesty's dominions in North America will require less encouragement Expanding this point, he declares that "the lands in question are excellent, the climate temperate; the native grapes, silk worms, and mulberry trees are everywhere; hemp grows spontaneously in the valleys and low lands; iron ore is plenty in the hills, and no soil is better adapted for the culture of tobacco, flax, and cotton than that of the Ohio." As to the ability of colonists to export these products, he says that on account of the navigable rivers produce can, by a land carriage of only forty miles, be sent cheaper from the Ohio country to Alexandria on the Potomac "than any kind of merchandise is at this time sent from Northampton to London;" moreover "large ships may be built on the Ohio, and sent laden with hemp, iron, flax, silk, to this kingdom."[3] Franklin concludes by declaring that there are already thirty thousand British subjects settled on the

[1] Franklin's Works, V., 44, 45.
[2] Ibid., p. 5.
[3] Ibid., pp, 47, 48.

Ohio lands, and asks if it is "fit to leave such a body of people lawless and ungoverned." With the capitol of Virginia at least four hundred miles distant how could the constitution and laws of that colony "be extended so as effectually to operate on the territory in question?" By Virginia laws all persons charged with capital crimes must be tried in Williamsburg. There is held the superior court and the General Assembly.[1]

Franklin's reply to the report of the Board of Trade was read to the council at the same time that Mr. Wharton made his argument. The council was fully convinced[2] and the Committee of Council for Plantation Affairs, on July 1st, 1772, reported to the King:—

"(1) That the lands in question had been for some time past and were then in an actual state of settling, numbers of families to a very considerable amount removing thither from his said Majesty's other colonies.

"(2) That the lands in question did not lie beyond all advantageous intercourse with the kingdom of Great Britain,"[3] and "that it was their opinion a grant should be made to Mr. Walpole and his associates,"[4] and "to the end that the several persons actually settled, or that might thereafter settle, might be more properly and quietly governed, the said settlement and district should be erected into a separate government."[5]

---

[1] Franklin's Works, V., 73, 74.

[2] Rev. William Hanna was present when the case of the company was presented to the council. He wrote to Sir William Johnson that after Mr. Walpole had made some pertinent observations, "Mr. Wharton spoke next for several hours and replied distinctly to each particular objection, and through the whole of the proceedings he so fully removed all Lord Hillsborough's objections and introduced his proofs with so much regularity and made his observations on them with so much propriety, deliberation, and presence of mind, that fully convinced every Lord present." Christopher Gist's Journal, p. 242.

[3] Franklin's Works, X., 355.

[4] Plain Facts, p. 153.

[5] Franklin's Works, X., 357. The Pennsylvania Chronicle, Nov. 14, 1772, published an article entitled "Reasons for Lord Hillsborough's Resignation," signed "An Advocate of Lord Hillsborough." The writer said that Mr. Walpole and others had petitioned for a grant " adjoining to the Mississippi with intention to establish a new colo-

On the 14th of August, 1772, *the King approved of this report*[1] "and ordered the Lords of Trade to report to him in Council, if any, and what terms of settlement and cultivation; and what restrictions and reservations were necessary to be inserted in the grant. . . . with a clause to save and preserve to the respective occupiers all prior claims within its limits. . . .; and also to prepare a plan for establishing a new government on the said lands, together with an estimate of the expense, and the ways and means by which the same should be defrayed by Mr. Walpole and his associates. The same day, the King in council, by a further order, gave the necessary directions to the Lords Commissioners for trade and plantations, for carrying the above into execution; and that the Earl of Dartmouth[2] should direct his Majesty's Superintendent for Indian affairs to apprise the chiefs of the Six Nations and their Confederates of his Majesty's intentions to form a settlement upon the lands which he purchased of of them in 1768. Accordingly the Earl of Dartmouth sent instructions to Sir William Johnson. . . . and in obedience thereto, the Six Nations were informed and much approved of the Settlement."[3]

The chiefs of the western tribes were assembled April 3d, 1773, at Scioto, and the same communication made to them. They appeared highly pleased and expressed a desire to take the new colonial governor, who ever he might

---

ny," and that Lord Hillsborough's "political reasons" against it were that Great Britain "depopulates very fast . . . and as to the utility of a new colony, granting that we could spare our people, no more advantage would accrue to Great Britain from this Mississippi establishment than if it was to take place in the confines of India." The Walpole grant is here perhaps confused with Gen. Lyman's Mississippi grant made about the same time. See Pennsylvania Gazette and Pennsylvania Chronicle, Feb. 24, 1773.

[1] Besides Plain Facts on this point, see also letter of Mr. Wharton to Col. Mercer, Aug. 20, 1772. Washington's Writings (Sparks) II., 485. Mr. Wharton says that the King ordered "That a new government should be established."

[2] Lord Dartmouth had succeeded to Hillsborough's position.

[3] Plain Facts, p. 153. The same facts in different language may be found in Franklin's Works, X., 357-360.

be, "by the hand and afford him all the assistance in their power."[1]

Meanwhile not the Indians alone, but the American people were hearing about the new colony. In June, 1772, Washington wrote: "The report gains ground that a large tract of country on the Ohio, including every foot of land to the westward of the Alleghany Mountains is granted to a company of gentlemen in England, to be formed into a separate government."[2] The following year the American newspapers published a good deal about the new colony and its progress.[3] Many particulars appeared in the *Pennsylvania Chronicle* of March 8 and the *Pennsylvania Gazette* of March 10 about the grant which "is to be granted to Thomas Walpole" and company, the latter paper publishing a statement that on account of obstacles which the scheme had met, it would, according to some letters, be brought before Parliament.

But there was no necessity for bringing the matter into Parliament. May 6, 1773, Lord Dartmouth (Hillsborough's successor) reported for the Board of Trade, which had been ordered to arrange particulars in regard to the land grant and colonial government. He said that, the establishment of the new colony was, they supposed, founded principally "on the necessity there was of introducing some regular form of government in a country incapable of participating the advantages arising from the civil institution of Virginia," and therefore they had given their attention first to "the form and constitution of the new colony which they named Vandalia."[4] We are unable to deter-

---

[1] Plain Facts, p. 154. For the entire speech returned by the western chiefs on that occasion see Considerations on the Agreement. . . with the Hon. Thos. Walpole, pp. 9, 10, 11.

[2] Washington to Lord Dunmore, Lieut. Gov. of Va., June 15, 1772. Washington's Writings (Ford), II., 353.

[3] See Pennsylvania Chronicle, Feb. 24, March 8, June 7, Sept. 20; Pennsylvania Gazette Feb. 24, March 10, June 9, Sept. 8; Pennsylvania Journal, June 9, July 21, Nov. 24, 1773.

[4] Plain Facts, p. 154. If the statements in the following letter were correct in regard to the name of the new colony, we should be tempted to use it for other interesting items.

mine many of the particulars concerning the form of government determined upon in this constitution.   Three years before, Thomas Pownall, a member of the Company and brother of the secretary of the Board of Trade, had proposed to take the Massachusetts Bay charter for a model,[1] and it seems likely that that plan was followed. The governor and other officers of the colony were to be appointed by, and hold "their several commissions during the pleasure of the King."[2]   These officers, moreover, were to be quite independent of everyone except the King in regard to their salaries.   They were to be paid by the Company, to be sure, but the Company was compelled to give bonds for £10,000 to secure them,[3] and later actually did give such security for the payment of £3,000 annually for officers' salaries.[4]   Beginning with the date of the governor's commission, the Company was to have paid that amount regularly in half yearly payments for the support of the governmental establishment.[5]   Walpole and his associates were to have been held responsible for such payment "until provision should have been made by some act of General Assembly, *to be approved of by his said Majesty*, for the support of the said establishment."[6]   The salaries of the new colonial officers were fixed by Lord Dartmouth's report as follows:

It is from "Mr. John Ballendine to his friend in Virginia," dated London, March 23, 1773. He says: "I can inform you for certain that the new province on the Ohiu is confirmed to the proprietors by the name of Pittsylvania, in honor of Lord Chatham. Mr. Wharton, from Philadelphia, will be appointed governor in a few days; all other appointments to be made by the King. The seat of government is to be fixed at the fork of the Great Kanawa and Ohio rivers, as I expected from the situation of the country." Pa. Journal, June 9, 1773. The Pennsylvania Gazette, Sept. 8, 1773, published a rumor that Col. George Mercer, who had been agent for the old Ohio Company, was "to be governor of the new colony on the Ohio, which should be called Pittsylvania."

[1] Thos. Pownall to Sir William Johnson, April, 1770. Writings of Washington (Sparks), II., 448.

[2] Considerations on the Agreement, et cetera, p. 36.

[3] Franklin's Works, X., 362.

[4] Considerations on the Agreement, et cetera, p. 36, citing Register "in the provincial rolls office."

[5] Franklin's Works, X., 362.

[6] Loc. cit. The italics are mine.

Governor	£1,000
Chief Justice	500
Assistant Judges	400
Attorney General	150
Clerk of the Assembly	50
Secretary	200
Two Ministers	200
	£2,500

Besides this the Company was responsible for the payment of the contingent expenses to an amount not to exceed £500.[1]

In view of these facts concerning the form of government, and the farther fact (to be shown presently) that the *colony* was to have embraced a considerably larger territory than the grant to the Company, it can hardly be asserted that a proprietary colony, in the ordinary meaning of that term, was contemplated. Indeed, none of the thirteen colonies were more dependent on the crown than it was intended that Vandalia should be. Speculation was, of course, indulged in as to who was to receive appointments to the new colonial offices,[2] and there is little doubt that George Mercer, former agent for the Ohio Company, expected to be appointed governor.[3]

But to return to Lord Dartmouth's report. It goes on to recommend "that the grantees should, upon the day of the date of the grant, pay into the receipt of his said Majesty's exchequer, the sum of £10,460:7s:3d., pursuant to the agreement made with his Majesty's treasury on the 4th of January, 1770," and that all prior claims upon the lands "should be saved and reserved to the respective occupiers and possessors."[4]

---

[1] Franklin's Works, X., 362.

[2] See, for example, note on p. 29.

[3] See his letter to William Fairfax, Dec. 2, 1773. Rowland's George Mason, I., 157.

[4] This would secure the titles of the so-called Indiana Co. (Traders grant), George Washington (see his advertisement in Pa. Chronicle of June 28, 1773) and other officers of the French and Indian War. As for the Ohio Company the facts seem to be as follows: When the Walpole company petitioned for a large grant early in 1770, it was found that not only was Arthur Lee's petition of 1768 for 2,500,000 acres of the same land being pressed in

In regard to the boundaries, the land grant to the company was to be bounded by the following lines: "Beginning at the south side of the river Ohio, opposite to the mouth of Scioto; then southerly through the pass of the Ouassioto[1] Mountains, to the south side of the said mountains; then along the side of the said mountains northeastly to the fork of the Great Kenhawa, made by the junction of Green Briar River and New River; thence along the said Green Briar River, on the easterly side of the same, unto the head or termination of the northeasterly branch thereof;

---

opposition, but also the Ohio Company, represented by Colonel George Mercer, was suing for a completion of their grant which also conflicted. (Franklin's Works, X., 350). The latter was bought off by the following written agreement, made May 7, 1770. "We, the Committee of the Purchasers of a Tract of Country for a new Province on the Ohio in America, do hereby admit the Ohio Company as a Company purchaser with us, for two Shares of the said Purchase in Consideration of the engagement of their Agent, Col. Mercer, to withdraw the application of the said Company for a separate Grant within the Limits of the said Purchase. Witness our Hands," et cetera.—Christopher Gist's Journal, p. 244. "This action of Mercer without authority was not approved by the Ohio Company, and while the subject was still in agitation the Revolutionary War came on and put an end to the existence of both Companies."— Dinwiddie Papers, I., 18. This is not strictly true, as will be shown. See George Mason's account of the Ohio Company's action in Rowland's George Mason, I., 414.

Arthur Lee and his associates failed to receive a grant. Besides Arthur Lee and two Londoners, his company comprised " thirty-three gentlemen of character and fortune in Virginia and Maryland, (several of whom were of his Majesty's council in Virginia, and many of them, members of the house of assembly, both of that colony and of the province of Maryland)." They gave themselves the name of " Mississippi Company" and proposed to increase their number to fifty. Considerations on the Agreement, et cetera, pp. 25, 26. This appears to have been a scheme distinct from that embodied in " a petition, that was presented to government in 1772, by many respectable persons, requesting the establishment of a new colony, at an expense to the crown, upon the river Mississippi." Dinwiddie Papers, I., 38. I find nothing further to show that this petition proposed a new government. Arthur Lee seems to have continued in a position of opposition to the Walpole Company. In August, 1782, he opposed in congress the doctrine that the sovereignty over the western lands devolved upon congress, urging that if congress should take that position, the claim of Franklin and others " to some of the lands in question" "will be strengthened." Rather than allow this, he thought that our ministers plenipotentiary in Paris, one of whom was Franklin himself, ought not to be allowed to claim the West in the pending peace negotiations on any other ground than the rights of the separate states. See The Thomson Papers, N. Y. Hist. Soc. Colls, 1878, p. 143; Welling's The States' Rights Conflict Over the Public Lands, Am. Hist. Assn. Papers, III. No. 2, p. 174.

[1] An old name for the Cumberland. See " A New Map of the Western Parts of Virginia, Pennsylvania, Maryland, and North Carolina " by Thos. Hutchins, London, November 1, 1778; also a map published by Laurie and Whittle, No. 53, London, 12th May, 1794. The pass referred to is evidently Cumberland Gap.

thence easterly to the Alleghany Mountains; thence along
the said Alleghany Mountains to Lord Fairfax's line; [1] thence
along the same to the spring head of the north branch of the
river Potomack; thence along the western boundary line of
the province of Maryland to the southern boundary line of the
province of Pennsylvania; thence along the said boundary
line of the Province of Pennsylvania to the end thereof;
thence along the western boundary line of the said province
of Pennsylvania until the same shall strike the river Ohio;
thence down the said river Ohio to the place of beginning." [2]
These are the limits of the land grant, but no restrictions
were made upon settling beyond a certain Cherokee treaty
line, [3] and in fact the western limits of the Colony of Vandalia were extended beyond the line of the grant to the
Louisa or Catawba, or Cuttawa river," [4] which is now
called the Kentucky river. [5]

There was one other item of the report which is of interest as showing the design to establish the Episcopal
church in the new colony. It provided that in each parish
" there should be a tract of three hundred acres reserved
for the purpose of a glebe for the support of a minister of
the church of England." [6]

Such, then, are the main points of Lord Dartmouth's report, drawn up by the Lord's Commissioners for trade and

[1] Lord Fairfax's boundary line ran from the S. W. corner of Maryland, S. E. by S. to
the headwaters of " Conway R." or " Rapid Ann." See Thos. Hutchins' Map, London,
Nov. 1, 1778.

[2] The language of Lord Dartmouth's report. Franklin's Works, X., 363, and Plain
Facts, p. 155.

[3] Established at the treaty of Lochaber, Oct. 1770. Franklin's Works, X., 366.

[4] Plain Facts, p. 156. Christopher Gist (Journal, p. 243) says that the new colony " contained within its limits all the Walpole Grant, with the addition of all the country westward to the Kentucky River." Professor Turner's map of Vandalia in the Americal Historical Review, Oct., 1895, represents, not the proposed colony of Vandalia, but merely
the proposed land grant to Walpole and company.

[5] Compare the following maps: " The U. S. of N. Am. etc." by Wm. Faden, 1783; Map
of Richardson and Urquhart, Lond., Apr. 26, 1780; " Carte de l'Amerique Septentrionale
etc." 1790; and Hutchins' Map, Lo nd., Nov. 1, 1778, on which the river in question is
called " Kentucke or Cuttawa River."

[6] Franklin's Works, X., 364.

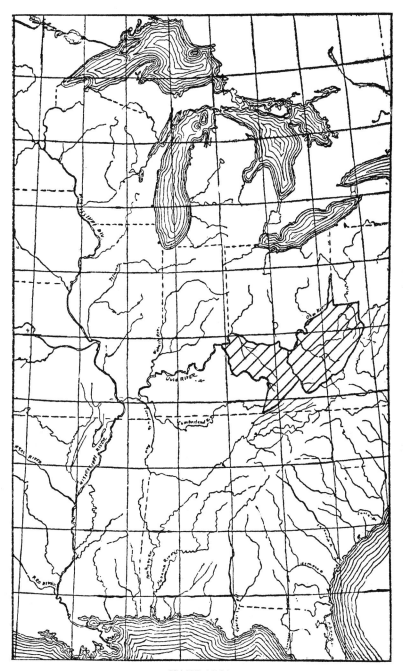

VANDALIA.

plantations in obedience to his Majesty's order of August 14, 1772, and presented May 6, 1773. May 19th, the King referred it to the lords of the Council. After a minor change had been made, by the attorney and Solicitor-General, concerning the manner of paying the quit rents, a decisive order was issued from the council chamber, October 28, 1773, directing the King's attorney and Solicitor-General to "prepare and lay before this Committee" of the Council "the draught of a proper instrument, to be passed under the Great Seal of Great Britain, containing a grant to the Honorable Thomas Walpole, Samuel Wharton, Benjamin Franklin," et cetera, "of the lands prayed for by their memorial, . . . inserting in the said draught the conditions and reservations proposed in the said report of the Lords Commissioners for trade and plantations, dated the 6th of May, 1773." [1] So the matter seemed to be settled. [2] When the governor of Virginia presumed to grant lands in the Vandalia territory, he was sharply reprimanded by Lord Dartmouth, then Secretary of State for the Colonies, [3] and the following spring was careful that no Virginia surveyors should enter any part of the territory "Petitioned for by Walpole and Company (commonly called the new Government)." [4]

But still the final papers, establishing the Walpole grant and the colony of Vandalia had not been executed; delayed, probably, by the threatening attitude of the old colonies. In the spring of 1775, the draught of the royal grant had been prepared, and even examined and corrected by mem-

[1] This order may be found in Plain Facts, p. 157, and Franklin's Works, X., 367.

[2] It had been rumored before this, that the new colony was about to be established. The Pa. Journal, November 24, 1773, published part of a letter from London, dated September 7, saying of the new colony, " in all probability the next packet will carry to America proper documents for its establishment." The Pa. Chronicle of September 20, published a letter assuring that " the draft for the charter for establishing a new colony on the Ohio . . . was in a few days to be carried up by Mr. Thurloe for the last revision of his Majesty in Council, previous to a final delivery of it to the Proprietors." Newspaper copies in Draper Collection, Clark MSS., Vol. 13, No. 1, p. 172.

[3] Plain Facts, p. 159; Franklin's Works, X., 369.

[4] Draper Colls., Preston Papers, IV., No. 6.

bers of the Company, when the execution of it was sus-
pended. [1] " The Lord President of his Majesty's Privy
Council requested that the Honorable Mr. Walpole and his
associates would wait for the grant aforesaid, and the plan
of government of Vandalia, until hostilities, which had
then commenced between Great Britain and the United
Colonies, should cease." [2] But those hostilities did not
cease until the thirteen colonies had won. If the war had
broken out a little later there seems every reason to suppose that there would have been fourteen instead of thirteen colonies to fight for independence. As it was, however, the colony of Vandalia failed of establishment. The
company lived on for a number of years, vainly petitioning
Congress to confirm its claims. [3]

   With the Declaration of Independence, Virginia had asserted claims to the back lands in accordance with the provisions of her old charter. She was much annoyed when
Congress "received and countenanced petitions from certain persons styling themselves the Vandalia and Indiana
Companies." [4] Congress seems never to have taken defini-
tive action on the Vandalia claims, and in a few years
nothing more is heard of the company which, in its day,
bid fair to become the pioneer in the political organization
of the west.

---

[1] Plain Facts, p. 159.

[2] Franklin's Works, X., 370. Thos. Walpole wrote to Wm. Trent, May 30. 1775, " We
must flatter ourselves that the little which is wanting here will soon be done." He also
said, " I hope that you will find everything in Vandalia in as good a way as you could
expect; if not you will be able to take such measures as may secure the property which
we have got there, and especially that you will be able to protect it from farther viola-
tions." Historical Magazine, 1857, Vol. I., p. 85. Whether this property was anything
more than the land, which was merely contracted for, it is impossible to say. It may
have been property formerly owned by the Ohio Company.

[3] Plain Facts, p. 160; Journals of Congress, Sept. 14, 1779. It was occasionally referred
to in connection with the Indiana, Illinois, and Wabash companies,—e. g. in Pennsylvania Packet, Jan. 5, 1786, quoting from a letter dated Dec. 10, 1781 from a Virginia
delegate in Congress.

[4] See the Remonstrance in Hening X., 557.

CHAPTER III.

CONCLUSIONS FROM THE FOREGOING CHAPTERS.

In the two preceding chapters it has been the endeavor
to give a connected history of the various attempts to establish colonial governments west of the Alleghany mountains. This history makes possible a few generalizations
here, by way of summary.

In the first place, it is worthy of note that practically
every proposition for a new colony involves its location on
the Ohio. Not only did the Ohio river flow through a most
fertile country, but it was in itself the gateway to the west.
It was natural that would-be western colonists should
turn their attention first in that direction.

In the next place, it is noticeable that the supporters of
these schemes are, for the most part men from Pennsylvania, or New Jersey. This is probably due to the following facts. Pennsylvania was one of the most populous colonies, the nearest to the Ohio, and was by her charter limited on the west. The inhabitants of most of the colonies
could find desirable lands without going outside of what they
considered their legal limits. The Hazard scheme was evidently Presbyterian in its conception and its support, and
so Hazard would naturally get a large following from Presbyterian New Jersey.[1]

Dr. Franklin's unwavering interest in new colonies
doubtless had some effect on Pennsylvanians, and without
doubt strongly influenced his son, Governor William Franklin of New Jersey; where also Thomas Pownall was Lieutenant Governor at the time of the Albany Congress. To
these facts should be added the information and interests

---

[1] Hazard argued that only Presbyterians can, and are willing to colonize. 4 Am. Archives, I., 863.

of the Pennsylvania Indian traders, such as the firm of Baynton, Wharton and Morgan.

Again, it may seem strange, that when all these schemes for new colonies were being brought forward, there was no protest from Virginia, that her jurisdiction was being threatened. Every scheme proposed, involved an invasion of territory, which, after the Revolution, she so strenuously insisted on as within her charter limits. In November, 1770, the Earl of Dunmore wrote to Lord Hillsborough that he had made it his "business to inquire and find out the opinion of the people" on the question of "establishing a colony on the Ohio." [1] His letter would indicate that he found only disapproval; but among all the objections advanced, not one had reference to the invasion of the jurisdiction of any old colony. We might surely have expected that Lord Hillsborough's letter to the Virginia governor, inviting objections to the establishment of Vandalia, back of Virginia, would have called out an objection on the score of invaded jurisdiction. But instead, the official reply states that "with respect to the establishment of a new colony on the back of Virginia, . . . when that part of the country shall become sufficiently populated it may be a wise and prudent measure," [2] the only care being that land titles under prior grants should be respected by the new colony. Also in the opposition arguments before the council at Whitehall, while the question was brought up as to the expediency of the western country, or part of it, being under Virginia's jurisdiction, the charter right of Virginia was, so far as we know, never mentioned as an objection to the establishment of Vandalia. There can be little doubt

[1] Documents Relative to the Colonial History of N. Y., VIII., 253. Also Fernow's Ohio Valley in Colonial Days, p. 276. George Washington declared in November, 1773, that Virginia had a right to the lands beyond " the western boundary of the new colony" both by charter and by sale of the Six Nations, thus virtually conceding the better right of the Vandalia Company to the lands that had been as yet merely bargained for. Washington to Gov. Dunmore, Writings (Ford) II., 396. Washington evidently thought the King's Proclamation of 1763 did not interfere with Virginia's territorial extent.

[2] Pres. Nelson to Lord Hillsborough, Oct. 18, 1770. Public Good, p. 24.

that it was generally recognized that the crown had the
right to cut off vacant .lands from any colony at pleasure,
regardless of that colony's chartered extent.   It was urged
that one object (quite a secondary one however) of the
King's proclamation of 1763, was to limit the colonies on
the west, as ''the charters of many of our old colonies give
them, with few exceptions, no bounds to the westward but
the South Sea.''[1] If so, the King was merely using his
recognized right.   In the previous century there had
been several cases in which new colonies had been
carved out of the chartered territory of older ones, and
there is no reason to believe that the crown did not still
possess the right.   In this connection, it may be well to
mention that the fact of the province of Quebec, being extended to the Ohio and Mississippi rivers by the Quebec
Act of 1774[2] was no guarantee whatever against new colonies being erected north of the Ohio, whenever the British government should choose to establish them.[3]

But the most difficult subject upon which to·draw conclusions from the foregoing attempts at colonization, is
the policy of the British government in regard to new
western colonies.   In order to understand the situation, it
is necessary to know something of the way American affairs were conducted in London.   Until 1766 their direction
appears to have been jointly in the hands of the Secretary
of State for the Southern Department, and the President
of the Lords Commissioners for Trade and Plantations,[4] the
other members of the Board cutting little or no figure.
The President of the Board of Trade doubtless attended to
most of the details of colonial administration, but as the

---

[1] Annual Register, 1763, p. 20. The Annual Register is supposed to have been written
by Edmund Burke.

[2] Houston's Const. Docs. of Canada, p. 91.

[3] It is Hinsdale's opinion that one object of the Quebec Act was '' permanently to
sever the West from the shore colonies, and put it in train for being cut up when the
time should come, into independent governments that should have their affiliations with
the St. Lawrence basin rather than with the Atlantic slope.'' Old Northwest, p. 141.

[4] Commonly called the Board of Trade.

colonies were also within the Secretary's department, the latter often exercised a marked influence in colonial affairs. Important questions, however, were referred through the King to the Council, with whom rested practically the final decision.

In 1766 a change was introduced. The Board of Trade was made " a mere Board of Report upon reference to it for advice or information on the part of the Secretary of State," and "Shelburne, who held the seals of the Southern depart ment, was directed to carry it out in conjunction with Hillsborough, the President of the Board."[1] Another change was made January 20, 1768, when Lord Hillsborough became Secretary of State for the Colonies, the creation of this new office being found necessary on account of the growing importance of colonial affairs.[2] This made Hillsborough both President of the Board of Trade, and Secretary of State for the Colonies, with the whole direction of colonial affairs, subject to the King and Council. This was the situation when Thomas Walpole and Company began action for the Vandalia scheme, and remained the situation until the summer of 1772, when Horace Walpole could write as follows: "Not a cloud in the political sky except a caprice of Lord Hillsborough, who is to quit his American Seals because he will not reconcile himself to a plan of settlement on the Ohio which all the world approves."[3] He did resign, and was succeeded by Lord Dartmouth, who was, or at least had been regarded as, friendly to "settlement on the Ohio."[4]

Lord Hillsborough, however, before his resignation, took such a prominent part in the question of new colonies, that his real personal influence needs to be considered. The slurring language of Horace Walpole is not the only indi-

---

1 Fitzmaurice, Life of Shelburne, II., 2. See this work for description of the system.

2 Dictionary of National Biography, XXVI., 428.

3 Horace Walpole to Sir Horace Mann, July 23, 1772. Letters of Horace Walpole (Cunningham), V., 401.

4 Franklin to his son, Sept. 12, 1766. Works, IV., 137.

cation that he was not held personally in high regard.
Franklin wrote of him to his son that he, "of all the men
I ever met with, is surely the most unequal in his treatment of people, the most insincere and the most wrong-
headed,"[1] and Franklin was not the man unfairly to dis-
parage another over whom he had won a signal triumph.
King George III. said "I am sorry to say, I do not know
a man of less judgment than Lord Hillsborough."[2] To be
sure, these opinions of the Earl's judgment, may, perhaps,
not have been generally held; but, putting them with the
fact that his report on the Vandalia matter was actually
rejected, much to his mortification, it is fair to presume
that the British government did not allow its colonial policy to be shaped by Lord Hillsborough. With this in
view it would certainly be wrong to base conclusions as to
British policy in regard to new colonies upon his opinion,
though it is not necessary to deny that he did have a certain influence upon it. Now with this understanding of
the administration of colonial affairs and the personal influence of Lord Hillsborough, let us examine what was
actually done, and what important opinions were actually
expressed by those in position to have a real influence upon
colonial policy.

It should be pointed out first, however, what has doubtless been quite apparent, that the whole question of new
colonies was bound up with the question of western land
grants and western settlement. At the court of St. James,
practically the whole question was one of western settlement; the idea of new colonial governments being, in the
main, merely incidental to it. No evidence appears to
show that until 1748[3] the British government was ever
called upon to form a policy as to trans-montane settlements. Then the Board of Trade reported to the Privy

---

[1] Franklin to his son, July 14, 1773, Works, V., 196.

[2] George III., to John Robinson, Oct. 15, 1776. Historical MSS. Commission, Tenth
Report, Appendix, Part VI., p. 15.

[3] Franklin's Works, V., 32.

Council "That the settlement of the country lying to the westward of the great mountains, as it was the centre of the British dominions, would be for his Majesty's interest, and the advantage and security of Virginia and the neighboring colonies."[1] The Council approved of this, and in the spring of 1749, not only was the grant to the Ohio Company authorized, but the instructions to the governor of Virginia expressed the hope that "such examples may likewise induce the neighboring colonies to turn their thoughts towards designs of the same nature."[2]

Soon, an even larger grant was given to another company. Clearer proof could not be asked to show that the British government in 1748 and 1749 was plainly favorable to settlements west of the Alleghany mountains. The object was, doubtless, to secure the back country from the French, and to get the Indian trade into English channels, but the fact nevertheless remains, that it was, at that time, the British policy to encourage settlement of the west. But the actual settlement was interrupted by the French and Indian War.

Great Britain, before the peace, was in a position to choose between the island of Guadaloupe and Canada with the west. After hesitation, the latter two were taken. But while the question was under discussion, Dr. Franklin published a reply to the arguments advanced against retaining Canada and the west. After discussing and dismissing the apprehension that the American colonies were becoming useless to the mother country, he said: "I shall next consider the other supposition that their growth may render them dangerous. Of this, I own, I have not the least conception, when I consider that we have already fourteen separate governments on the maritime coast of the continent; and, if we extend our settlements, shall probably have as many more behind them on the inland

---

1 Franklin's Works, V., 32.

2 Ibid., p. 33.

side." He argued that their numbers prevented the colonies from becoming dangerous to Great Britain. Their mutual jealousies prevented union "without the most grievous tyranny and oppression." Perhaps Franklin's argument had some weight in deciding the British government to retain Canada and the west instead of Guadaloupe.

Soon after the peace,[1] the King's proclamation was issued. His majesty ordered the organization of the governments of East and West Florida, Quebec and Granada; but the rest of the land just acquired from France was reserved "*for the present*," "for the use of the...Indians," "as also all the land and territories lying to the westward of the sources of the rivers which fall into the sea from the west and northwest." The king further declared; — "We do hereby strictly forbid on pain of our displeasure, all our loving subjects from making any purchases or settlements whatever, or taking possession of any of the lands above reserved *without our special leave and license for that purpose first obtained.*"[2]

Now what was the real object of this proclamation? The Annual Register, after remarking on the fact that the largest and best part of the conquered country had not been placed under any government, said: "Many reasons may be assigned for this apparent omission. A consideration of the Indians was, we presume, the principal, because it might have given a sensible alarm to that people, if they had seen us formally cantoning out their whole country into regular establishments. It was in this idea that the the royal proclamation of the 7th of October, 1763, strictly

---

[1] Canada Pamphlet, Works III., 111. Sparks says (Franklin's Works, IV., 1) that this " pamphlet was believed to have had great weight in the ministerial councils, and to have been mainly instrumental in causing Canada to be held at the peace." If this is true, Franklin's argument may have suggested the King's proclamation as the first step in a far-seeing plan which, admitting the inevitable settlement of the west, proposed to limit at once the colonies " on the maritime coast," *contemplating* the existence of " as many more behind them on the inland side "— the whole object being to reduce America to the then condition of the German empire, i. e., many and weak governments, rather than few and strong ones. This is, however, merely conjecture.

[2] Franklin's Works, V., 80.

forbids . . . any extension of our old colonies beyond
the heads of the rivers. . . ."[1] Washington wrote in
1767, "I can never look upon that proclamation in any
other light (but this I say between ourselves) than a temporary expedient to quiet the minds of the Indians. It
must fall, of course, in a few years, especially when those
Indians consent to our occupying the lands."[2] But probably the very best authority for the purpose of the proclamation was George Grenville, prime minister of Great
Britain when it was issued. He "always admitted that the
design of it was totally accomplished, so soon as the country was purchased from the natives."[3] This evidence would
indicate that the proclamation was merely "a temporary
expedient" and that it was not contemplated to place a
permanent check on western settlement. This view is supported, too, by the words of the proclamation itself, which
says that the west is reserved *"for the present . . .* for
the use of the Indians;" orders all settlers to remove from
all "lands, which, *not having been ceded to, or purchased by,
us,* are still reserved to the Indians;" forbids private persons to purchase lands of the Indians, but when the latter
"should be inclined to dispose of the said lands, *the same
shall be purchased* only for us;" and that none of "our loving subjects" may take possession of any of the land in
question "without *our special leave and license* for that purpose first obtained."[4] Why not accept as the object of the
restrictions the reason given in the proclamation; viz., that
the Indians "should not be molested or disturbed in the
possession of such parts of our dominions and territories
as, not having been ceded to, or purchased by, us, are reserved to them."[5]

---

[1] Annual Register, 1773, p. 20.

[2] Washington-Crawford Letters (Butterfield), p. 3.

[3] Franklin's Works, V., 37.

[4] Franklin's Works, V., 80. The italics are mine.

[5] Ibid., p. 79. Professor Coffin says there seems to be no reason for doubting that

Franklin argued for that view in his successful reply to Hillsborough. The latter contended in 1772 that the "two capital objects" of the proclamation were to restrict the settlements to territory where they could be kept in due subjection to the home government, and also within reach of the trade and commerce of Great Britain.[1] Hillsborough was first made President of the Board of Trade in September, 1763, and so was in position to know its object when the proclamation was issued.

Between the two views, supported as they are, it is impossible to come to a definite conclusion; but considering Hillsborough's alleged "insincerity," the contradictory statements of the then prime minister, and the fact that not the Board of Trade, but the Council had the real decision of questions of policy, is it not probable that Hillsborough's view was wrong? It is quite possible indeed that Hillsborough from the first, intended one thing, while the British government, as a whole, intended something quite different. And we must finally conclude from the evidence at hand that the probable object of the King's proclamation was to quiet the Indians and keep settlers off the unpurchased lands leaving the final disposition of those lands to the future. This view is borne out by subsequent facts.

Three years had scarcely passed after the issuing of the proclamation when the Illinois scheme was agitated and was "really approved" by Lord Shelburne, Secretary of State,[2] who had a control of colonial affairs independent, at that time, of the Board of Trade. The matter, however, was "referred to the Board of Trade for their opinion" by the King in council.

A great object of colonization was, of course, "to pro-

---

the proclamation is what it appears to be. The Province of Quebec and the Early American Revolution, p. 415. But see his interpretation, pp. 398-431, and especially p. 428.

[1] Ibid., p. 4.

[2] See above, p. 18.

mote and extend the commerce of Great Britain." When
the scheme was referred to the merchants by the Board
of Trade, they declared unanimously that if colonies were
established at Detroit and in the Illinois country, they
would promote and extend the said commerce. With this
decision the argument that the new colonies would not
meet the great end for which colonies were established,
could hardly stand.[1] Indeed the evidence[2] indicates that
up to the time Lord Hillsborough was made both President of the Board of Trade and Secretary of State for the
colonies, the British government was favorable to the Illinois scheme. Soon after that, Franklin wrote, " Counsels
are so continually fluctuating here that nothing can be depended on."[3] This doubtless has reference to the death
of Townsend, the illness of Pitt, Hillsborough's promotion,
and various changes in the ministry during 1768. It was
probably due to these changes that the Illinois scheme
failed. Its failure is some evidence that British policy was
at that time opposed to western colonization.

In the fall of that same year, however, the British government bought, for a considerable sum, the claims of the
Six Nations to a vast tract of land west of the Alleghany
mountains. Why was that purchase made if it was the
British policy to restrict all settlement to the region east
of the mountains? The purchase is strictly in accordance
with the theory of the King's proclamation advanced
above.

Finally, we see the British government convinced that
the establishment of the Vandalia colony would be for the
advantage of Great Britain, and the papers for its erection actually drawn up. So we may say that at last it was
British policy to establish at least one new colony west
of the Alleghany mountains.

---

[1] Notice, in this connection, Lord Clare's opinion in regard to the fur trade. See
above, p. 19.

[2] See above, pp. 18, 19.

[3] See above, p. 19.

That the British ministry expected to exert a strong influence in the establishment and operation of whatever new western governments might be established, there can be no doubt. Of course, too, unauthorized settlements beyond the reach of governmental authority could scarcely meet British approval, as tending only to cause Indian uprisings. Lord Dartmouth, writing to Dunmore in September, 1774, and speaking of the British policy "from the Royal Proclamation of 1763 down to the present time, said: "It has been the invariable Policy of this Country to prevent, by every possible means, any Settlement of the King's subjects in situations where they could not fail of exciting the jealousy of and giving dissatisfaction to the Indians, and where at the same time the Settlers would be out of reach either of the control or protection of the King's Government." [1] This, of course, could not be applied to establishments under conditions similar to those of the proposed Vandalia, else Dartmouth could hardly have called the policy "invariable."

But to sum up all the evidence, what was the British western policy during the third quarter of the eighteenth century? It may have been a consistent one; but from the evidence at hand, we are not able definitely to affirm that it was, for we are still unable to tell the reasons for the King's proclamation and the final failure of the Illinois scheme. Indeed with the many ministerial changes made during the period, [2] one could hardly expect a consistent policy. Then too, there was doubtless more or less indiffer-

---

[1] Mass. Hist. Colls. X., 725. Cf. Dunmore's reply in Clark MSS. (Draper Colls.) XV., 4.

[2] The ministerial changes were especially frequent during the first decade of George III's reign. Notice the following prime ministers:—

1757, Newcastle-Pitt coalition.

1761, Newcastle (Pitt resigned).

1762, Bute.

1763, George Grenville.

1765, Rockingham.

1766, Chatham.

1767, Grafton.

1770, Lord North.

ence to a subject which must have seemed insignificant to ministries unable to stand long, even by applying them-selves closely to what must have seemed, to them much more important business. But, taking all things into con sideration, we may conclude that the British government, during the period considered, was in the main, not unfavor-able to western settlement under certain regulations. As to new colonial establishments, the Illinois scheme was the first one presented to the government.[1] The favorable re-ceipt of that scheme, and the actual success of the Vanda-lia scheme, as well as the general favor shown to the land companies, all point to the same attitude with respect to new colonies.

As to what would have been the subsequent policy in regard to the west, if the Revolutionary War had not in-terfered, it is, of course, impossible to say.[2] Considering the somewhat uncertain policy pursued before the war, it is not unlikely that some change in the ministry might have introduced a complete change of policy. But when we consider the rapid extension of unlawful settlement beyond the mountains, before the war, in spite of British efforts to prevent it, we see that had there been no Revolution, that same western movement would have continued with con-stantly increasing force, whether made lawful or not, be-yond the limits of Vandalia. The establishment of some kind of government throughout the west would, in time, have been found absolutely necessary. The same argu-ments which were used to secure approval of the Vandalia scheme, would have been used again, and the Vandalia case urged as a precedent. If, instead of cutting the whole west up into new colonies of the size of Vandalia, it had

---

[1] Report of the Board of Trade, March, 1768. Franklin's Works, V., 5.

[2] Thomas Paine in his Public Good (p. 27) which appeared in 1780, distinguishes three kinds of lands at the commencement of the Revolution, the third of which were those "held in reserve whereon to erect new governments and lay out new provinces as ap-pears to have been the design." Paine presents something of an argument for this proposition, but in my opinion fails to prove it.

been annexed to various old colonies, as the Northwest was annexed to Quebec, by the Quebec Act of 1774, such an arrangement would very probably have been merely temporary. As the country became settled, the British government would have found it advisable to cut up the country into smaller divisions, and a political geography would have resulted in the west similar to that which may be seen today in Canada, or Australia. The beginning of the Revolution saw Great Britain embarked on a course which, but for that war, must have led, perhaps indirectly, but nevertheless, considering the circumstances and forces at work, almost inevitably, to the cutting up of the west into many separate governmental establishments.

CHAPTER IV.

TRANSYLVANIA.

In spite of the numerous schemes already described, to establish new colonial governments beyond the Alleghanies, the west saw nothing done towards the actual erection of such a government until 1775. In that year there appeared in the west, for the first time, a new establishment which it was proposed to develop into a new government—an establishment which, for a time, was a new and an independent government. It seems probable that the company which set up this new government intended originally to petition for a royal grant and charter, as the Walpole company had done. It was probably thought that the British government, which had already decided favorably in the case of Vandalia, could easily be induced to grant the new company an equally extensive territory just west of the Vandalia colony.[1] As for the Indian title, which stood in the way, the plan seems to have been to buy it from the Cherokees before applying for a grant. At any rate, when the Louisa Company (as the Transylvania Company was first called) was formed at Hillsborough, North Carolina, August 27, 1774, the members signed an agreement "to rent or purchase a certain Territory or Tract of Land . . . from the Indian Tribes now in possession thereof, and do bind and oblige ourselves and our heirs each to furnish his

---

[1] In their Memorial to Congress, Sept. 25, 1775, the proprietors " flatter themselves that the addition of a new Colony, in so fair and equitable a way, and without any expense to the Crown, will be acceptable to His Most Gracious Majesty, and that Transylvania will soon be worthy of his Royal regard and protection." 4 Am. Archives, IV., 554; N. C Col. Records, X., 258.

Quota of Expenses necessary towards procuring a grant[1]
and settling the country."[2] At that time the company was
composed of Richard Henderson, John Williams, Thomas
Hart, Nathaniel Hart, John Luttrell and William John-
ston. Not very long afterwards, James Hogg, David Hart,
and Leonard Henly Bullock, were admitted and the name
"Transylvania Company" assumed.[3] There was a tradition
that Patrick Henry and Thomas Jefferson desired to join
the company, but that Colonel Henderson preferred not to
have them admitted "lest they should supplant the Colonel
as the guiding spirit of the company."[4] Patrick Henry
himself declared that Henderson invited him to join, but
he "uniformly refused and plainly declared his strongest
disapprobation of their whole proceedings."[5] At all
events the membership of the company seems to have remained confined to the nine men mentioned above, all from
North Carolina.

In the spring of 1775, the Cherokee chiefs were gathered
to meet Henderson and his friends at Watauga, in what is
now northeastern Tennessee. After considerable parley,
a treaty was executed March 17th. In consideration of several loads of merchandise, valued at £10,000, the Cherokees
deeded the territory bounded as follows: "Beginning on
the said Ohio River at the mouth of Kentucky, Ehenoca or
what, by the English, is called Louisa River, from thence
running up the said River and the most northwardly fork
of the same to the head spring thereof, thence a South East

---

[1] This might possibly be taken as meaning a grant from the Indians merely, and
indeed the cession which the company finally obtained was sometimes called "the great
grant," but it was not customary to apply that term to an Indian cession. Moreover we
would expect the Company to be planning to get a crown grant, as differences between
the colonies and the mother country had not at that time reached the point where
separation was expected.

[2] Draper Colls., Ky. MSS., I.

[3] Ibid.

[4] Extracts from Jas. Alves's Henderson Papers, in Draper Colls. Kentucky MSS., II.

[5] Patrick Henry's deposition, made at Williamsburg, June 4, 1777. Draper Colls., Kentucky MSS., I. This deposition shows that Patrick Henry was concerned in another
scheme to purchase lands from the Cherokees.

course, to the top ridge of Powels' mountain, thence west-
wardly along the ridge of the said mountain unto a point
from which a north west course will hit or strike the head
spring of the most Southwardly branch of Cumberland
River, thence down the said River, including all its waters,
to the Ohio River, thence up the said River as it meanders
to the Beginning."[1] As the meaning of the phrase "including all its waters" has been subject to some dispute, it
may be well to notice what those present at the treaty supposed it to mean, or in other words, what they regarded as
the southern boundary of the cession. In 1777 and 1778 a
number of depositions in regard to the Watauga treaty were
taken by Virginia authorities. One man who was there declared, under oath, that in his opinion the boundary line
"was to keep the dividing Ridge between Cumberland" and
Tennessee Rivers.[2] Another man, under oath, gave some
particulars of the treaty. He said that after some parley-
ing, "The Indians then agreed to sell the land as far as
Cumberland River, and said Henderson insisted to have
Cumberland River and the waters of the Cumberland river,
which the Indians agreed to."[3] The depositions of other
men describe the southern boundary in the same language
as the deed, while there seems to be no evidence that anyone present at the treaty regarded that boundary to be the
Cumberland River merely.[4] Major Pleasant Henderson[5] described the southern boundary as a westerly line crossing
"the Cumberland mountains so as to strike the ridge which
divides the waters of the Tennessee River from those of the
Cumberland, and with that ridge to the Ohio River."[6] So
we see that at the time,[7] the watershed between the two

[1] See attested (1803) copy from the original, and also the complete copy of the Watauga treaty in Draper Colls. Kentucky, MSS., I., Butler's Kentucky, pp. 503–506.

[2] Deposition of Chas. Robertson, Oct. 3, 1777,—Draper Colls., Kentucky, MSS., I.

[3] Deposition of Jas. Robinson,—Ibid.

[4] See Depositions in Draper Colls., Kentucky MSS., I.

[5] Brother of Richard Henderson.

[6] Copy of Pleasant Henderson's MS., Draper Colls., Kentucky MSS., II.

[7] The petition from the inhabitants of Kentucky, presented to the Virginia House of

rivers seems to have been regarded as the southern boundary of the cession, as indeed one would naturally suppose
from the phrase "including all its waters." [1]   It is however,
undeniable, that the Cumberland River was, in 1785 and
afterwards, officially recognized as "the southern boundary
of the lands sold to Richard Henderson & Co.;" [2] but in
mapping the outlines of the territory over which the Transylvania Company claimed, and (as much as any civilized
government of the time) exercised jurisdiction, and which
was called Transylvania, [3] it seems more reasonable to take
the natural interpretation of the deed [4] supported as it is by
the depositions of men present at the treaty, and the plain
statement of Richard Henderson's brother.   The so-called
"path-deed" was secured by Henderson and Company at
the same time, so that they might have territorial connection with the old colonies, but as the comparatively small
piece of land thus obtained was not considered a part of
Transylvania proper and was not called Transylvania [5] it
need not be considered here.

Delegates, Oct. 8, 1776, described the territory as extending "from the southernmost
waters of the Cumberland river." Journal of Virginia House of Delegates, Oct. 8,
1776, (Copy in Draper Colls., Clark MSS., XIV., p. 162.)

[1] C. C. Royce (Report of the Bureau of Ethnology, 1883-4, p. 149) says: "Although a
literal reading of these boundaries would include all the territory watered by the Cumberland River and its branches, the general understanding seems to have been . .
that Henderson's purchase did not extend south of the Cumberland River proper."

[2] Report of treaty commissioners to Richard Henry Lee, Pres. of Cong., Dec. 2, 1785;
and later, letter of Gen. Knox, Sec. of War, to Pres. of the U. S.—Am. State Papers,
Indian Affairs, I., 39.

[3] See, in this connection, the complaint of James Davis,—Draper Colls., Kentucky
MSS., II.

[4] Those who have taken the other view have failed to map correctly that part of the
southern boundary of Transylvania, which is less ambiguous in the deed, viz., the line
running along the ridge of "Powels' Mountain . . . unto a point from which a northwest course will hit or strike the head spring of the most Southwardly branch of the
Cumberland River." C. C. Royce (map accompanying Rep. of Bureau of Ethnology,
1883-4) evidently assumes the boundary as conceded later by the U. S. treaty commissioners. Professor Turner (map accompanying his article in Am. Hist. Rev., Oct., 1895,
appears to have followed Royce. Why the U. S. treaty commissioners should have conceded so much to the Cherokees does not appear. There is some doubt as to what range
was referred to by "Powels' mountain." Royce admits that this is uncertain. The
range that is called the Clinch Mountains best accords with the boundary description,
and was not unlikely the range referred to.

[5] Deposition of Nathaniel Henderson, Oct. 27, 1778, Draper Colls., Kentucky MSS., I.

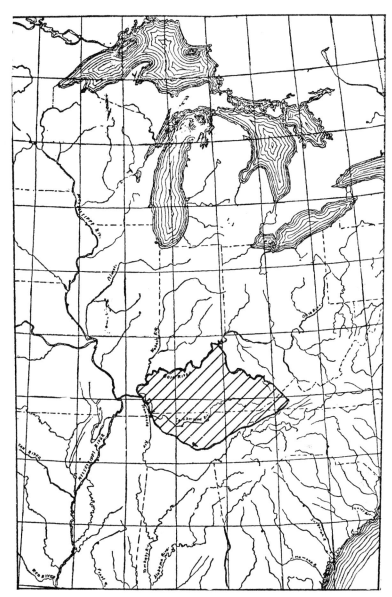

TRANSYLVANIA

One point is noticeable in regard to the northeastern boundary, viz. : that it is for most of its length, the same as the southwestern boundary of Vandalia. Evidently Henderson well understood what the Vandalia boundary was, and planned that his colony should join on the southwest.

But to return to the actual progress of the company. In spite of Governor Dunmore's proclamation, issued March 21, 1775, calling upon all civil and military officers "to use their utmost endeavors to prevent the unwarrantable and illegal designs of the said Henderson and his abettors," and ordering that if he or anyone else should refuse to depart from lands within the limits of Virginia which were held by no other than an Indian title, "he or they be immediately fined and imprisoned in the manner the laws in such cases direct"[1]—in spite of this proclamation and opposition also on the part of the governor of North Carolina[2] the number of Transylvania settlers, already considerable for the time, kept on increasing.

✓ The Indians having shown a hostile disposition, Daniel Boone, who appears to have been looking after Henderson's interests in Transylvania, wrote to him, " . . . My advice to you, sir, is to come or send as soon as possible. Your company is desired greatly, for the people are very uneasy, but are willing to stay and venture their lives with you . . . "[3] But Colonel Henderson was already on his way west and reached Fort Boone (Boonesborough)

It is also shown by the fact that the deed for the "great grant" only was exhibited to the Transylvania legislature, Henderson at the time requesting that an entry of it be made in the journal, showing the extent of Transylvania "including the corners and abutments of the lands or country contained therein, so that the boundaries of our colony may be fully known and kept on record."—Journal of the Proceedings of the House of Delegates, et cetera. Collins, Kentucky, II., 506; Butler's Kentucky, p. 513.

[1] Dunmore's proclamation, Draper Colls., Kentucky MSS., I.; 4 Am. Archives, III., 1385; N. C. Col. Records, X., 308. See also Dunmore's letter of same date to William Preston directing that copies of the proclamation be scattered "throughout the Back Country," Draper Colls., Preston Papers, IV., No. 6.

[2] North Carolina Colonial Records, X., 273, 323.

[3] Collins's Kentucky, II., 498.

April 20th.[1] He had already settled on a form of government for his proprietary. He referred to it in his journal
entry for April 4, saying, "This plann is exceeding simple
and I hope will prove effectual. 'Tis no more than the
peoples sending Delegates to act for them in Gen[l] Convention." The need of some kind of civil government was becoming every day more apparent. Before he had been
among the settlers three weeks Henderson seized a favorable opportunity and addressed them on the subject of
government. The following entry in his journal, May 8th,
tells us about all we know of what may perhaps be called
the constitution of Transylvania, and the manner in which
it was adopted and put in operation. "Our plan of Legis-
lation, the evils pointed out — the remedies to be applied,
&c., &c., &c , were acceeded to without Hesitation — The
plann was plain & simple — 'twas nothing novel in its es-
sence a thousand years ago it was in use, and found by
every years' experience since to be unexceptionable — We
were in four distinct settlemt[s] Members or delegates
from every place by free choice of Individuals they first
having entering into writings solemnly binding themselves
to obey and carry into Execution such Laws as representatives should from time to time make, concurred with by a
Majority of the Proprietors present in the Country — The
reception this plann met with from these Gen[t]., as well as a
Capt. Floyd, a leading man in Dicks river settlement, gave
us great pleasure, and therefore immediately set ab[t]. the
business, appointed Tuesday the 23[d] Instant at Boonsbo'[gh],
and according made out writings for the different Towns
to sign and wrote to Cap[t]. Floyd appointing an Election
&c. Harrodsburgh & the Boiling spring settlem[ts] Rec[d]
their sum. Verbally by the Gen[t]. afs[d]. "

By this quasi constitution, the proprietors became the
executive branch of the government, with the power of ab-

---

[1] See Henderson's "Journal of an expedition to Cantuckey in 1775" in Draper Colls.
Kentucky MSS., I. Extracts are printed in Collin's Kentucky, II., pp. 498-501.

solute veto.   The company insisted on that point because
otherwise "the delegates of any Convention that might be
thereafter held would have it in their power to destroy the
claim of the proprietors."[1]   At least the first legislative ap-
portionment was also in the hands of the proprietors, who
gave directions that six members be returned from Boonesborough, three from Harrodsburgh,[2] four from Boiling
Spring, and four from St. Asaph.[3] The "Convention" met
on the day appointed under a great elm tree, and after
electing officers who were approved by the proprietors,
listened to a speech from Henderson. He declared that
laws were "indispendably necessary," and "we have a
right to make such laws without giving offense to Great
Britain, or any of the American colonies; without disturb-
ing the repose of any society or community under Heaven."[4]
He then recommended various subjects as suitable for legis-
lation.   The following laws were passed:

1. Establishing courts of judicature.
2. Regulating a militia.
3. To punish criminals.
4. Against swearing and Sabbath breaking.
5. For writs of attachment.
6. Ascertaining clerk's and sheriff's fees.
7. To preserve the range.
8. To improve the breed of horses.
9. For preserving game.

Besides passing these laws, eighteen articles of agreement
between the proprietors and the representatives were drawn
up and approved by both. They were little more than an
elaboration of Henderson's "plann." One article provided
for annual election of delegates, and another to add another
branch to the legislature; viz.—a council, "after the

---

[1] Deposition of Nathaniel Henderson. Draper Colls., Kentucky MSS., I.

[2] For some reason four were actually returned from Harrodsburgh.

[3] "Journal of the Proc. of the House of Delegates or Representatives of the Colony of
Transylvania."—4 Am. Archives, IV., 548; Butler's Ky., p. 506; Collins' Ky., II., 501.

[4] Journal of the Proceedings. Collins' Kentucky, II., 502; Butler's Kentucky, p. 508.

strength and maturity of the colony will permit." But this council should not exceed "twelve men possessed of landed estate who reside in the colony." [1] All this was important business, but five days was all the time required to transact it by this pioneer legislature of the west. It adjourned May 27, "in good order, everybody pleased." [2] The adjournment was to the first Thursday of the following September, but the "Convention" never met again.

Henderson remained awhile in Transylvania and then returned home. A meeting of the proprietors was held at Oxford, Granville Co., North Carolina, Sept. 25, 1775. [3]

At this meeting, James Hogg was appointed to represent Transylvania in the Continental Congress then sitting at Philadelphia. At the same time a memorial to Congress was drawn up, reciting the impossibility of calling a convention of the settlers in time to elect a delegate to that Congress, but engaging their concurrence in the selection of Mr. Hogg. The memorialists "hope and earnestly request that Transylvania may be added to the number of the United Colonies, and that James Hogg, Esq., be received as their delegate and admitted to a seat in the honourable the Continental Congress." Mr. Hogg reached Philadelphia, October 22. He soon wrote back, "You would be amazed to see how much in earnest all these speculative gentlemen are about the plan to be adopted by the Transylvanians. They entreat, they pray, that we may make it à free Government." [4]

Samuel and John Adams were friendly to the new colony but feared that it would increase the complications with the King, with whom the Congress hoped to become reconciled, by protecting "a body of people who have acted in de-

---

[1] Journal of the Proceedings, Collins's Kentucky, II., 507; Butler's Kentucky, p. 13 These eighteen articles might be called the completed Transylvania constitution.

[2] Henderson's Journal, May 27.

[3] See Minutes of this meeting including the memorial to Congress, in 4. Am. Archives, IV., 553 et seq.; N. C. Col. Records X., 256 et seq.

[4] Hogg to Henderson, 4. Am. Archives, IV., 545. Hogg adds that "many of them advised a law against negroes."

fiance of the King's proclamations,"[1] Silas Deane of Connecticut said he would send agents to look the country
over, and thought, if their report were favorable, many
Connecticut people would emigrate to Transylvania; but he
would have nothing to do with it unless pleased with the
form of government.[2]

To Jefferson and Wythe, Hogg said nothing of his pretentions to seat in Congress, but told them that the
Transylvania Company had sent him to announce their
"friendly intentions towards the cause of liberty." Hogg reports that Jefferson said it was his wish to see a free government extending back of Virginia to the Mississippi if
properly united to that colony, but he would not consent
that Transylvania should be acknowledged by Congress
until a Virginia Convention had approved of it. He
thought, however, that the approval of the next Convention
might be obtained if the Company would send one of their
number to present the case.[3] That Convention was indeed
appealed to, but not in a way that promised well for the
company. A petition with eighty-eight signatures came
from the inhabitants and "intended settlers" of Transylvania. The petitioners complain that they were allured to the
country by the easy terms of settlement and the "indefeas-
ible title" which they were assured the Company was able
to make. Now they are alarmed by the advance of the
purchase price from 20 shillings to 50 shillings per hundred
acres,[4] and the fear that his Majesty will not confirm the
Company's title in view of the fact that the land had been
previously ceded to the crown from the Six Nations, who
had claimed to be the sole possessors of the territory as far as
the Tennessee river. They "expect and implore to be taken
under the protection of the honorable Convention of the

---

[1] Hogg to Henderson, 4. Am. Archives, IV., 544.

[2] Ibid., p. 545.

[3] Ibid., p. 544.

[4] This advance was determined upon by the proprietors at their meeting at Oxford,
Granville Co., N. C., Sept. 25, 1775.

Colony of Virgina, of which we cannot help thinking ourselves still a part, and request your kind interposition
in our behalf that we may not suffer under the rigorous
demands and impositions of the gentlemen styling themselves proprietors."[1] The petition closes with the request
that, should the case be thought to come more properly
before "the General Congress," the Convention would in-
struct the Virginia delegates "to espouse it as the cause of
the colony."

Meanwhile the Transylvania company was exercising the
executive power in their little commonwealth. John Williams, a member of the company, wrote from Harrodsburg,
March 3rd, 1776, that there had been "some disturbances
and dissatisfaction among the people" (referring evidently
to what had called out the above petition), but "they were
trifling and hardly worth mentioning."[2] Writs of election
were issued for another "Convention" to sit at Harrodsburg, April 10th, and this time it was intended that the
inhabitants of Powell's Valley should elect delegates also.[3]
But some of the Transylvanians feared that "the proprietors would wish to establish some laws which might operate to their disadvantage," and requested that the "Convention" might be postponed until a "few men of better
abilitys come among them to assist in making such laws."[4]
The proprietors assented to this on their promising faith-
fully to observe the laws passed at Boonesborough the
year before, and the election was postponed.[5] It is not
improbable that this postponement was desired so as
to await the return of George Rogers Clark, who had gone
to Virginia in the previous fall. While there he sounded
public opinion on the Transylvania affair and made some
interesting plans. He tells them in his memoir as follows:— "While in Virginia I found there was various op-

---

[1] 4 Amer. Archives, VI., 1528; Collin's Kentucky, II., 510.
[2] John Williams to Col. J. Martin. Draper Colls., Clark MSS., XVI., p. 54.
[3] Ibid.
[4] Ibid.
[5] Ibid.

pinions Respecting Henderson Claim. many thought it
god, others douted whether or not Virginia could with
propriety have any pretentions to the Cuntry.   this was
what I wanted to know.   I immediately fixed on my plans,
that of assembling the people, get them to elect deputies
and send them to the assembly of Virginia, and treat with
them Respecting the Cuntry.   If Valuable Conditions was
procured, to declare ourselves Citizens of the state; otherways Establish an Independant Government, and by giving away great part of the Lands and disposing of the Remainder otherways we could not only gain great numbers
of Inhabitants, but in good measure protect them to carry
this scheam into effect." [1]

Returning west in the spring of 1776, Clark proceeded
with his plan.   He called the people to a general meeting
at Harrodsburg, June 6th, without announcing its object.
It happened that Clark himself was unable to reach Harrodsburg until evening of the appointed day.   The people,
according to Clark's account, had been in confusion for
some time, but at length had concluded that the object of
the meeting was to elect delegates to the Virginia Assembly
and draw up a petition asking that they be received into
that body, and that the Transylvania settlements be organized into a county of Virginia.   Clark found the election of
delegates too far advanced to change to the principle of
deputies with authority from the people to treat with another power.[2]   Clark himself, and J. G. Jones were elected
delegates to the Virginia Assembly, and in a few days set
out for Williamsburg.   They carried with them "The
Humble Petition of the Inhabitants of Kentucke (or Louisa)
River on the Western parts of Fincastle County,"[3] which
made complaints against Henderson and Company similar to

---

[1] Clark's Memoir. The original document is in Draper Colls., Clark MSS., XLVII.,
pp. 1 et seq. I have copied from it as he wrote it, merely adding punctuation.

[2] Clark's Memoir, p. 2.

[3] This petition may be found in Draper Colls., MSS., XIV., p. 148. On p. 154, ibid., is
"The Humble Petition of the committee of West Fincastle of the Colony of Virginia,
etc." Both petitions are to the same purpose.

those of the former petition, and expressed the hope that Clark and Jones would be received as delegates in the Assembly.

Before reaching Williamsburg, the delegates learned that the Assembly had adjourned, Jones turned back, but Clark kept on hoping to get some powder from the Virginia authorities for use in "Kentucke." Governor Henry "appeared much disposed to favour the Kentuckyins," but the council giving him a rather doubtful reception, Clark returned the order for 500 pounds of powder which was to be merely loaned "as to Friends in distress," and decided to return home and organize an independent government.[1] He told the Council that he "was sorry to find that we should have to seek protection elsewhere, which I did not doubt of getting."[2] This threat alarmed the Council, and the powder was at once given outright and even transported freely as far as Pittsburg.[3]

The Virginia Assembly met in the fall. Clark and Jones were refused seats, probably because of their irregular election before the organization of Kentucky County. Colonel Richard Henderson was there working vigorously to prevent such an organization. But in spite of this and other opposition,[4] a bill was finally passed to organize the new county of Kentucky. December 21, 1776, the Council ordered that commissions be issued to county officers for Kentucky.[5]

So a large part of "the colony of Transylvania" became peaceably incorporated into the state of Virginia. After

[1] Clark's Memoir, p. 7.

[2] Ibid. Where Clark thought of seeking protection is not clear. There is an interesting correspondence on the subject between William Wirt Henry and L. C. Draper (Clark MSS., XVI., pp. 91-94) in which the former thinks Clark intended to appeal to the Spaniards, while Draper thinks that nothing more is meant than a threat to set up an independent government.

[3] Ibid.

[4] A member from Fincastle County was also much opposed, as he wished Kentucky to be annexed to his own county. Clark's Memoir, p. 7.

[5] Journal of the Va. Council, Dec. 21, 1776.— Draper's manuscript copy in Clark MSS., XVIII., p. 13.

struggling for nearly two years, Richard Henderson succeeded in getting for his Company a large compensatory
grant on the Ohio and Green rivers.[1] North Carolina ap-
propriated the remainder of what was considered the Henderson purchase, giving the company a grant in Powell's
Valley; "and thus vanished the golden dream of Richard
Henderson and Company."[2]

If a different course had been followed — the course
which Clark planned to follow in case the settlements had
declared their independence, viz.: giving away much of
the land and selling the rest at a low figure, besides allow-
ing the people a more liberal government — then the self-
interest of settlers would probably have led them to con-
tinue that support of the proprietors and their measures
which they seem to have given at first. The absence of
marked opposition from the Virginia patriots to an independent and liberally governed Transylvania is noticeable.
The framers of Virginia's first constitution plainly contemplated the erection of a new government within their charter limits west of them.[3] The state government even
expressed grave doubts as to whether the Assembly would
be willing to receive Kentucky,[4] whose people were freely
offering themselves to Virginia. This seeming indifference
on the part of Virginia would, if continued, have materially
aided the Transylvanians in maintaining independence, if
they had persisted in it. An independent Transylvania, or
an independent Kentucky led by George Rogers Clark,
during the Revolutionary War, might have made a marked
difference in subsequent American history, particularly if
the colony had allied itself with Spain, or adhered to Great
Britain in the struggle. In either case the United States
would probably have been limited at the peace to the ter-

---

[1] Littell's Laws of Kentucky, III., 587; Hening, IX., 571.

[2] Nathaniel Hart (whose father was a member of the Company) to Mann Butler,
October. 1833.   Draper Colls., Kentucky MSS., II.

[3] Va. Const. of 1776. Hough's Am. Const., I., 430; Poore's Constitutions, II., 1912

[4] Clark's Memoir. p. 6.

ritory east of the Alleghany mountains.   Had the country
not been united to Virginia as it was, its history would
most likely have been similar to that of Vermont — really
much in sympathy with the American cause and continually knocking at the doors of Congress for admission to
the Confederacy; but, if not getting it, taking position as
a quasi independent and sovereign state, holding aloof, and
ready to join with which ever side should come out victor
in the contest.[1]

---

[1] It will be attempted to show in a later study that this was the attitude of Vermont
during a large part of the Revolutionary War.

CHAPTER V.

NEW STATE SCHEMES PRIOR TO 1780.

Thus far we have had to do with schemes for new British colonies. With the Declaration of Independence the idea of i ew colonies gives place to that of new states. The change was, however, by no means a sharply defined one. One attempt to set up a new government began probably before American independence was declared. It involved the region about the head-waters of the Ohio, which was claimed by both Pennsylvania and Virginia, and incorporated by the latter as a part of West Augusta county. The scheme was set on foot in June or the beginning of July, 1776, by David Rogers, (who was a member of the Virginia Assembly), and others.[1] Certain definite boundaries were proposed and a memorial exhibited to several persons at Pittsburg.[2] The people were directed to "choose men to meet and Consult whither application should be made to Congress for laying off the country within the said limits into a new Government or whether they would not immediately proceed to Colonize themselves by their own authority, and send Delegates to Congress to represent them." [3]

Another proposition was that the people "on the Western Waters" should decide whither a "joint Petition of the Inhabitants" should be presented to Congress "praying their Interposition in settling the Disputes which have occasioned

[1] Memorial of the Committee of West Augusta to the Va. House of Delegates.—Va. Senate Journal, Oct. 30, 1776. MS. copy in Draper Colls., "Pa., N. Y., Va., O., Ky., and Tenn. Papers," IV., 32.

[2] Ibid. Among the "Yeates Papers," owned by the Historical Society of Pennsylvania, there is a draft of this memorial, but in certain particulars it differs from the one apparently presented to the Virginia House of Delegate.

[3] Ibid.

our Unhappiness" or whether they should take things into their own hands "by our immediately colonizing ourselv[es] by our own Authority, and sending our Delegates to the said Congress to represent us as the fourteenth Link in the American Chain."[1]   It was "recommended to the different Districts on the Western Waters to meet....and give their free Voice which of these Modes is most agreeable, and it is hoped that the Minority will generously give up to the Majority; and if a Majority is found in Favour of the former Mode all will sign the said Petition, and if a Majority is found in Favour of the latter that all will acquiesce then and there in Choice of two Members for a Convention to be held at Becket's Fort four Days after such Election for the express Purpose of forming a new Mode of Government for the intended new Colony Choosing two Members to represent us in Congress, Laying out the said Colony in Counties, and issuing their Summon's for calling an Election of legislative & Executive Officers agreeable to the Plan of Government so formed."[2]

Whether this meeting was ever held we do not know. In July, Rogers and others refused to take an oath prescribed by the Virginia convention and "persisted in using all their influence to make proselytes to their favorite scheme of a new Government."[3] By the first of August a petition to Congress was in circulation.[4] That document pointed out the evils to which the petitioners were subjected on account of the conflicting claims of Pennsylvania and Virginia to jurisdiction over them, and the "embarrassing and perplexing" land claims of George Croghan, and the Indiana and Vandalia companies. The petitioners say they are "neither Politicians nor Orators," but "are at least a rational and Social People. They have "emigrated from

---

[1] MS. copy in possession of the State Historical Society of Wisconsin.
[2] Ibid.
[3] Memorial of the Committee of West Augusta.
[4] Crumrine (Hist. of Wash. Co., Pa., p. 187) proves this date from a letter of Jasper Yeates to James Wilson, July, 1776.

almost every Province of America." but "having imbibed
the highest and most extensive Ideas of Liberty," they
"will with Difficulty Submit to the being annexed to or
Subjugated by (Terms synonimous to them) any one of those
Provinces, much less the being partitioned or parcelled
out among them." They protest that they will not "Suffer
themselves, who might be the happiest & perhaps not the
least useful Part of the American Confederacy as forming
a secure, extensive & Effectual Frontier and Barrier against
the Incursions, Ravages & Depredations of the Western
Savages, to be Enslaved by any set of Proprietary or other
Claimants. or arbitrarily deprived and robbed of those
Lands & that Country to which by the Laws of Nature &
of Nations they are entitled as first Occupants, . . . whilst
the Rest of their Countrymen softened by Ease, enervated
by Affluence & Luxurious Plenty, & unaccustomed to Fa-
tigues, Hardships, Difficulties or Dangers, are bravely con-
tending for and exerting themselves on Behalf of a Consti
tutional, natural, rational & social Liberty." They contend
that "no Country or People can be Either rich, flourishing,
happy or free . . . . . whilst annexed to or dependent on
any Province, whose Seat of Government is those of Pennsylvania & Virginia, four or five hundred Miles distant,
and separated by a vast, extensive & almost impassible
Tract of Mountains, by Nature itself formed and pointed
out as a Boundary between this Country and those below
it."

The memorialists request finally, "that the said Country
be constituted. declared and acknowledged a separate, distinct & independent Province & Government, by the Title
& under the Name of 'The Province & Government of
Westsylvania', be impowered & enabled to form such Laws
and Regulations & such a System of Polity & Government,
as is best adapted & most agreeable to the peculiar Neces-
sities, local Circumstances & Situation thereof, and its Inhabitants invested with every other Power, Right, Privi-

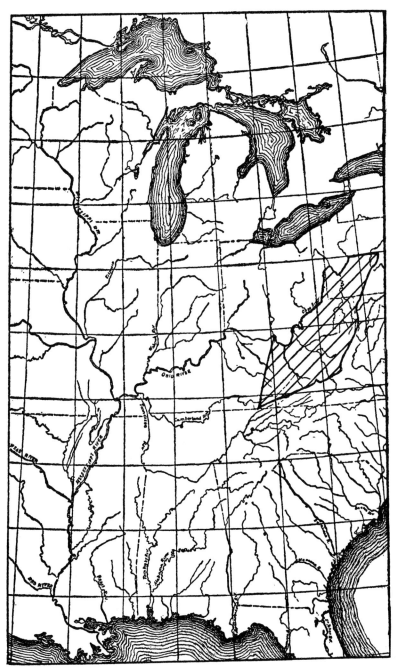

WESTSYLVANIA.

lege & Immunity, vested or to be vested in the other
American Colonies; be considered as a Sister Colony, &
the fourteenth Province of the American Confederacy, that
its Boundaries be: Beginning at the Eastern Branch
[bank] of the Ohio opposite the Mouth of the Scioto,
and running thence in a direct Line to the Owasioto Pass,
thence to the Top of the Allegheney Mountain, thence with
the Top of the said Mountain to the Northern Limits of
the Purchase made from the Indians in 1768, at the Treaty
of Fort Stanwix aforesaid, thence with the said Limits to
the Allegheney or Ohio River, and thence down the said
River ...... to the Beginning." [1]

Such was "The Memorial of the Inhabitants of the Country West of the Allegheney Mountains." [2] They claimed that
at least 25,000 families had settled within the above boundaries since 1768. But in spite of these numbers and the argu-
ments of the petitioners Congress gave them no encouragement. Indeed there is no evidence that Congress even
considered the petition.

But before the year was out another proposition for a
new western state was on its way to Congress. Silas
Deane, writing from Paris Dec. 1, 1776, to the Secret
Committee of Congress, made suggestions about the western lands. He thought the tract between the Ohio, Mississippi, and the Great Lakes might, if managed properly,
be made to defray the whole expense of the war. [3] In
order to enhance its value a new government should, he
suggested, be planted "at the mouth of the Ohio, between
that and the Mississippi." [4] A grant "equal to two hundred miles square" should be given " to a company formed
indiscriminately of Europeans and Americans, which company should form a distinct state, confederated with and

---

[1] The State Historical Society of Wisconsin has a complete copy of this petition
taken from a copy among the Yeates Papers in possession of the Historical Society of
Pennsylvania.

[2] The petition was so entitled.

[3] Silas Deane to Secret Committee of Congress. 5 Am. Archives, III., 1021.

[4] Ibid., p. 1021.

under the general regulations of the United States General of America." This company should consist of at least one hundred persons, and receive its grant on condition that within seven years it should have a certain number of families settled on the land and a civil government established, "regulated and supported on the most free and liberal principles, taking therein the advice of the honorable Congress of the United States of America."

Deane's scheme further provided that the new state should not be taxed until it had a thousand families, when it should contribute to "the publick expenses of the continent, or United States" in proportion to its population and "be entitled to a voice in Congress."[1] We have seen that about a year before this Silas Deane was much interested in the Transylvania undertaking.[2] James Hogg thought then that he was meditating settling in their new colony himself with a party of Connecticut adventurers.[3] It is not improbable then, that when he suggested to the secret committee of Congress the advisability of planting a new state in the West, he hoped to take a prominent part in its affairs himself. If his recommendation had been acted upon, and a grant given to "a company formed indiscriminately of Europeans and Americans," he, as agent of Congress in Paris, was in good position to enlist the Europeans in the enterprise. But, so far as we know, the suggestion of Silas Deane was never even considered by Congress, and he himself, if he ever had the idea of molding a new state government and wielding a strong power in it, must have soon abandoned it.

In conclusion, it needs only to be pointed out that in spite of the fact that every one of the numerous schemes to form governments west of the Alleghany mountains had failed,

---

[1] Silas Deane to Secret Committee of Congress, Dec. 1, 1776. 5 Am. Archives, III., 1021.

[2] See above, p. 58. See also his long letter to James Hogg, laying down liberal principles of government which he thought a new colony should adopt. 4 Am. Archives, IV. 556; N. C. Col. Records, X., 300-304.

[3] Hogg to Henderson. N. C. Col. Records, X., 376.

some few giving promise for a time of ultimate success, but most of them meeting with little or no real encouragement from the first — in spite of this there had been, when Congress took up the subject, a pretty constant agitation of the question throughout the whole preceeding quarter century. During that time the American people as a whole must have contemplated more than once the possibility of new governments being set up in the West. Although the idea received a check when the back land was all claimed as within the legal limits of certain of the thirteen states, and it was not generally held that Congress had succeeded to the right of the crown to carve out new governments in the west at will, nevertheless the statesmen of the Revolution could hardly have come finally to the task of dealing with the west without remembering something of those attempts, and being influenced by the fact that until then there had been a widespread expectation that separate governments on a political equality with those of the sea-board, would in time be established beyond the mountains. It was another question which brought Congress to take its first action in favor of new states, but had that action not been taken at that time, and had the old states held on to the western land, it must have been recognized sooner or later, that the West had not gained its proportionate share in the liberty acquired by the Revolution, that concerning the local colonial governments which had been expected, the West had plainly lost by the Revolution. We may fairly say that the schemes for new western governments prior to congressional action on the subject, served as a not unimportant factor in ushering in that action.

BIBLIOGRAPHY.

Albach, James R.   Annals of the West. Pittsburgh, 1858.

American Archives: 4th series, 6 vols., 1837–46; 5th series, 3 vols., 1848–53. By Peter Force. Washington.

American State Papers, Vols. IV. and V.; Indian Affairs, Vols. I. and II. Washington, 1832–34. Gales and Seaton.

Annual Register, or a view of the History, Politics, and Literature for the Year 1763. London, 1776.

Butler, Mann.   History of the Commonwealth of Kentucky. Cincinnati, 1836.

Chalmers, George, Esq., F. R. S., S. A.   Opinions of Eminent Lawyers on various points of English Jurisprudence. London, 1858.

Clark MSS. Draper Collections, State Historical Society of Wisconsin, Madison.

Coffin, Victor. The Province of Quebec and the Early American Revolution. Bulletin of the University of Wisconsin. Economics, Political Science and History series, Vol. I., No. 3. Madison, Wis., 1896.

Collins, Lewis and his son, Richard H. History of Kentucky. 2 vols. Covington, Ky., 1874.

Colonial Records of North Carolina. Collected and edited by William L. Saunders, 10 vols. Raleigh, 1886–90.

Considerations on the Agreement of the Lords Commissioners of His Majesty's Treasury, with The Honourable Thomas Walpole and the associates for Lands upon the River Ohio in North America, in a letter to a member of Parliament. [Supposed by Ford (Bibliography of Franklin) to be written by Benjamin Franklin.] London, 1774.

Constitutions, Colonial Charters, and other Organic Laws of The United States. Compiled by Ben: Perley Poore. 2 parts. Washington, 1877.

Crumrine, Boyd. History of Washington County, Pennsylvania. Philadelphia, 1882,

Dinwiddie, Robert. The Official Records of. 2 vols. (In Va. Hist. Soc. Colls.) Introduction and notes by R. A. Brock. Richmond, Va.

Documents Relative to the Colonial History of the State of New York. 14 vols. Albany, 1857.

Draper, L. C. MS. Life of Boone. 5 vols. Draper Collection, State Historical Society of Wisconsin.

Expediency of securing our American Colonies by Settling the country adjoining the River Mississippi, and the country upon the Ohio, Considered. (MS. copy) Edinburgh, 1763.

Fernow, Berthold. The Ohio Valley in Colonial Days. Albany, 1890.

Fitzmaurice, Lord Edmund. Life of William, Earl of Shelburne. 3 vols. London, 1875-76.

Frank Cowan's Paper. Greensburg, Pa., 1873.

Franklin, Benjamin. Complete Works. Compiled and edited by John Bigelow. 10 vols. New York and London, 1887-88.

Franklin, Benjamin, The Works of B. Franklin Containing Several Political and Historical Tracts. . . . With Notes and a Life of the Author. By Jared Sparks. 10 vols. Boston, 1840.

Gee, Joshua. The Trade and Navigation of Great Britain Considered. London, 1730.

Gist, Christopher. Christopher Gist's Journals with historical, geographical and ethnological notes and Biographies of his Contemporaries. By Wm. M. Darlington. Pittsburgh, 1893.

Grenville Papers. 4 vols. London, 1853.

Hening, William Waller. Statutes at Large. 13 vols. New York, Richmond and Philadelphia, 1819-23.

Hinsdale, B. A. The Establishment of the First Southern Boundary of the United States. In Am. Hist. Ass'n. Report, 1893.

Hinsdale, B. A.   The Old Northwest.   New York, 1888.

Hinsdale, B. A.   "Western Land Policy of the British." In "Ohio Archaeological and Historical Quarterly" for Dec. 1887. Columbus, 1887.

Historical Magazine for 1857, Vol. 1.   Boston and London, 1857.

Historical Manuscripts Commission, Tenth to Fourteenth Reports.   London, 1885–96.

Holmes, Abiel.   American Annals or a Chronological History of America.   2 vols.   Cambridge, 1829.

Hough, Franklin B.   American Constitutions.   2 vols. Albany, 1872.

Houston, William.   Documents Illustrative of the Canadian Constitution.   Toronto, 1891.

Journals of Congress.   Published by order of Congress. Philadelphia, New York, etc.

Keith, Sir William, Bart.   A Collection of Papers and other Tracts written occasionally on various subjects. London, 1740.

Kentucky MSS.   25 vols.   1772–1782.   Draper Collection, State Historical Society of Wisconsin.

Littell, William, Esq. The Statute Law of Kentucky. 3 vols. Frankfort, 1809–11.

Massachusetts Historical Collections.   10 vols. Boston, 1852–71.

McMaster, John Bach.   A History of the People of the United States.   4 vols.   New York, 1884–95.

Newspaper Extracts. 4 vols. 1752–1794. Draper Collections, State Historical Society of Wisconsin.

Paine, Thomas.   The Political and Miscellaneous Works of Thomas Paine.   2 vols.   London, 1819.   (Including Public Good.)

Pennsylvania Archives.   Selected and arranged by Samuel Hazard.   Philadelphia, 1854.

Pennsylvania Chronicle and Universal Advertiser. 3 vols. 1768–74.

Pennsylvania Gazette. 34 vols.   Philadelphia, 1728–89.

Pennsylvania Journal. 13 vols. Philadelphia, 1751-88.

Pennsylvania Packet and General Advertiser. 9 vols. Philadelphia, 1772-84.

Pennsylvania, New York, Virginia, Ohio, Kentucky and Tennessee Papers. 10 vols. 1747-1852. Draper Collection, State Historical Society of Wisconsin.

Perkins, James H. Annals of the West. Cincinnati, 1846.

Peyton, J. Lewis. History of Augusta County, Virginia Staunton, Va., 1882.

Plain Facts. Philadelphia, 1781. (According to Sabin's Dictionary, written by Benjamin Franklin or A. Benezet.)

Pownall, Thomas. The Administration of the Colonies. London, 1768.

Preston Papers. 7 vols. Draper Collection, State Historical Society of Wisconsin.

Public Records of the Colony of Connecticut. 15 vols. Hartford, 1850-90.

Remembrancer, or Impartial Repository of Public Events for the Year 1776. 2 parts. London, 1776-77. Printed for J. Almon.

Sato, Shosuke. History of the Land Question in the United States. Johns Hopkins University Studies, Fourth Series. Baltimore, 1886.

State of the British and French Colonies in North America. London, 1755.

Turner, Frederick J. Western State-Making in the Revolutionary Era. In *American Historical Review*, Oct. 1895 and Jan. 1896.

Walpole, Horace, Earl of Orford. The Letters of. Edited by Peter Cunningham. 9 vols. London, 1861.

Washington, George. The Writings of. Collected and edited by W. C. Ford. 14 vols. New York and London, 1889-93.

Washington, George. The Writings of George Washington. 10 vols. Edited by Jared Sparks. Boston, 1834.

Washington-Irvine Correspondence. By C. W. Butterfield. Madison, 1882.

The First American Frontier

AN ARNO PRESS/NEW YORK TIMES COLLECTION

Agnew, Daniel.
A History of the Region of Pennsylvania North of the
Allegheny River. 1887.

Alden, George H.
New Government West of the Alleghenies Before 1780. 1897.

Barrett, Jay Amos.
Evolution of the Ordinance of 1787. 1891.

Billon, Frederick.
Annals of St. Louis in its Early Days Under the French
and Spanish Dominations. 1886.

Billon, Frederick.
Annals of St. Louis in its Territorial Days, 1804-1821. 1888.

Littel, William.
Political Transactions in and Concerning Kentucky. 1926.

Bowles, William Augustus.
Authentic Memoirs of William Augustus Bowles. 1916.

Bradley, A. G.
The Fight with France for North America. 1900.

Brannan, John, ed.
Official Letters of the Military and Naval Officers of the
War, 1812-1815. 1823.

Brown, John P.
Old Frontiers. 1938.

Brown, Samuel R.
The Western Gazetteer. 1817.

Cist, Charles.

Cincinnati Miscellany of Antiquities of the West and Pioneer History. (2 volumes in one). 1845-6.

Claiborne, Nathaniel Herbert.

Notes on the War in the South with Biographical Sketches of the Lives of Montgomery, Jackson, Sevier, and Others. 1819.

Clark, Daniel.

Proofs of the Corruption of Gen. James Wilkinson. 1809.

Clark, George Rogers.

Colonel George Rogers Clark's Sketch of His Campaign in the Illinois in 1778-9. 1869.

Collins, Lewis.

Historical Sketches of Kentucky. 1847.

Cruikshank, Ernest, ed,

Documents Relating to Invasion of Canada and the Surrender of Detroit. 1912.

Cruikshank, Ernest, ed,

The Documentary History of the Campaign on the Niagara Frontier, 1812-1814. (4 volumes). 1896-1909.

Cutler, Jervis.

A Topographical Description of the State of Ohio, Indian Territory, and Louisiana. 1812.

Cutler, Julia P.

The Life and Times of Ephraim Cutler. 1890.

Darlington, Mary C.

History of Col. Henry Bouquet and the Western Frontiers of Pennsylvania. 1920.

Darlington, Mary C.

Fort Pitt and Letters From the Frontier. 1892.

De Schweinitz, Edmund.

The Life and Times of David Zeisberger. 1870.

Dillon, John B.

History of Indiana. 1859.

Eaton, John Henry.
Life of Andrew Jackson. 1824.

English, William Hayden.
Conquest of the Country Northwest of the Ohio. (2 volumes in one). 1896.

Flint, Timothy.
Indian Wars of the West. 1833.

Forbes, John.
Writings of General John Forbes Relating to His Service in North America. 1938.

Forman, Samuel S.
Narrative of a Journey Down the Ohio and Mississippi in 1789-90. 1888.

Haywood, John.
Civil and Political History of the State of Tennessee to 1796. 1823.

Heckewelder, John.
History, Manners and Customs of the Indian Nations. 1876.

Heckewelder, John.
Narrative of the Mission of the United Brethren. 1820.

Hildreth, Samuel P.
Pioneer History. 1848.

Houck, Louis.
The Boundaries of the Louisiana Purchase: A Historical Study. 1901.

Houck, Louis.
History of Missouri. (3 volumes in one). 1908.

Houck, Louis.
The Spanish Regime in Missouri. (2 volumes in one). 1909.

Jacob, John J.
A Biographical Sketch of the Life of the Late Capt. Michael Cresap. 1826.

Jones, David.
A Journal of Two Visits Made to Some Nations of Indians on the West Side of the River Ohio, in the Years 1772 and 1773. 1774.

Kenton, Edna.
Simon Kenton. 1930.

Loudon, Archibald.
Selection of Some of the Most Interesting Narratives of Outrages. (2 volumes in one). 1808-1811.

Monette, J. W.
History, Discovery and Settlement of the Mississippi Valley. (2 volumes in one). 1846.

Morse, Jedediah.
American Gazetteer. 1797.

Pickett, Albert James.
History of Alabama. (2 volumes in one). 1851.

Pope, John.
A Tour Through the Southern and Western Territories. 1792.

Putnam, Albigence Waldo.
History of Middle Tennessee. 1859.

Ramsey, James G. M.
Annals of Tennessee. 1853.

Ranck, George W.
Boonesborough. 1901.

Robertson, James Rood, ed.
Petitions of the Early Inhabitants of Kentucky to the Gen. Assembly of Virginia. 1914.

Royce, Charles.
Indian Land Cessions. 1899.

Rupp, I. Daniel.
History of Northampton, Lehigh, Monroe, Carbon and Schuykill Counties. 1845.

Safford, William H.
The Blennerhasset Papers. 1864.

St. Clair, Arthur.
A Narrative of the Manner in which the Campaign Against the Indians, in the Year 1791 was Conducted. 1812.

Sargent, Winthrop, ed.
A History of an Expedition Against Fort DuQuesne in 1755. 1855.

Severance, Frank H.
An Old Frontier of France. (2 volumes in one). 1917.

Sipe, C. Hale.
Fort Ligonier and Its Times. 1932.

Stevens, Henry N.
Lewis Evans: His Map of the Middle British Colonies in America. 1920.

Timberlake, Henry.
The Memoirs of Lieut. Henry Timberlake. 1927.

Tome, Philip.
Pioneer Life: Or Thirty Years a Hunter. 1854.

Trent, William.
Journal of Captain William Trent From Logstown to Pickawillany. 1871.

Walton, Joseph S.
Conrad Weiser and the Indian Policy of Colonial Pennsylvania. 1900.

Withers, Alexander Scott.
Chronicles of Border Warfare. 1895.

DATE DUE

30 505 JOSTEN'S